Featherstone

TIME TO COMMUNICATE

Communication and Language in the Early Years: How to observe, assess and plan for progress

TRUDI FITZHENRY
AND KAREN MURPHY

Featherstone
An imprint of Bloomsbury Publishing Plc

50 Bedford Square   1385 Broadway
London   New York
WC1B 3DP   NY 10018
UK   USA

www.bloomsbury.com

Bloomsbury is a registered trademark of Bloomsbury Publishing Plc

First published 2015

Photography © Shutterstock, LEYF,
and Rebecca Skerne, Stamford Bridge Primary School, ERYC

British Library Cataloguing-in-Publication Data
A catalogue record for this book is available from the British Library.

ISBN:
PB 978-1-4729-1928-1
ePDF 978-1-1929-8

Library of Congress Cataloging-in-Publication Data
A catalog record for this book is available from the Library of Congress.

10 9 8 7 6 5 4 3 2 1

Printed and bound in India by Replika Press Pvt Ltd.

This book is produced using paper that is made from wood grown in managed, sustainable forests. It is
natural, renewable and recyclable. The logging and manufacturing processes conform to the environmental
regulations of the country of origin.

With thanks to the staff and pupils at LEYF for their help with the photographs in this book.

To view more of our titles please visit www.bloomsbury.com

Contents

Introduction

Children are good communicators from birth. They use the skills available to them to express their needs, desires and interests. The development of good communication skills is necessary for children to be able to form friendships and is essential for later learning across the curriculum, especially in the areas of literacy and numeracy. The children's community charity I CAN reveals that approximately 1 million children across the United Kingdom begin formal schooling with a significant delay in their communication and language skills, which may hamper their ability to learn effectively.

As practitioners and parents we play a key role in the development of clear and effective communication. We are the child's earliest role models and what they see, hear and feel when we communicate with them shapes their own speaking, listening and wider communication skills. It has long been noted that children learn from what they experience in life, and this is especially true in the context of communication. If a child is listened to, they will feel valued and will learn to listen to others in turn. If a child is spoken to and time is taken to explain the world around them as they experience it, they will learn to be curious, ask questions and develop a rich vocabulary based on what they have heard. If a child sees the adults around them reading for pleasure and for information, they will see books, newspapers and magazines as a source of knowledge and enjoyment. Similarly, if a child sees others drawing, writing and communicating through the printed or typed word, they will learn the power of putting thoughts, ideas and beliefs down on paper for others to see.

When planning any adult-led activity, practitioners should consider which language and communication skills each child needs to be able to gain from it, and should structure the activity appropriately. For example, consider a shorter story time for those who find listening and understanding difficult, and always review the chosen book for suitable vocabulary and plot before reading it with the children.

As with the other books in this series, the ideas and activities in this book have been linked to the developmental bands of the Early Years Foundation Stage. Some of the outcomes have few or no statements so some sections have been combined; an example being 'writing' where birth to 11 months, 8-20 months and 16-26 months have been presented as a section on 'mark making'. Where there are assessment statements they have been included in the appropriate progress checklist at the end of the developmental stage.

This book is designed for practitioners to use as an assessment tool and guide as they observe, assess and support children's early communication, language and literacy skills.

How to use this book

This book supports the planning cycle at each stage of development. It contains clear guidance on what to observe and how to assess what is seen through both the assessment notes and progress checklists. Practical ideas to use in planning each child's individual next steps are also provided.

Each chapter in this book is linked to a phase or stage of development from birth to 60+ months. Each section is colour coded and links the Early Years Outcomes to the planning cycle, including observations, assessments and planning. Also included are possible links to the Characteristics of Effective Learning. Some of the photographs also contain a milestone comment: these are additional indicators of what we feel children may be able to demonstrate during this period.

There are also additional activities that offer the busy practitioner a wealth of ideas to choose from, that are linked to that specific age and stage of development. A short glossary features in each chapter and defines key terms as they appear. These definitions explain how the words and phrases should be interpreted within the book. A traditional alphabetical glossary of all terms used appears at the back of the book for quick reference.

The progress checklists at the end of each chapter are available for practitioners to use when observing children's communication skills. It is intended that the progress checklists could also be used alongside a setting's current tracking system to highlight any areas of concern and demonstrate progress made. They can be used to demonstrate progress in a specific area over time. The progress checklist at 40 – 60+ months is closely linked to the Early Learning Goal (ELG). It can be used to support the practitioner's professional judgement as to whether a child is at emerging, expected or exceeding level at the end of the Foundation Stage.

It is important that practitioners are aware of their responsibility to encourage parents to contact their health care professional if the child appears to be developing outside of the normative range. If there is little or no progress after they have spoken to parents and included timed specific interventions in the child's individual plan, then practitioners should seek parental permission to involve outside agencies.

Chapter 1
0 – 11 months

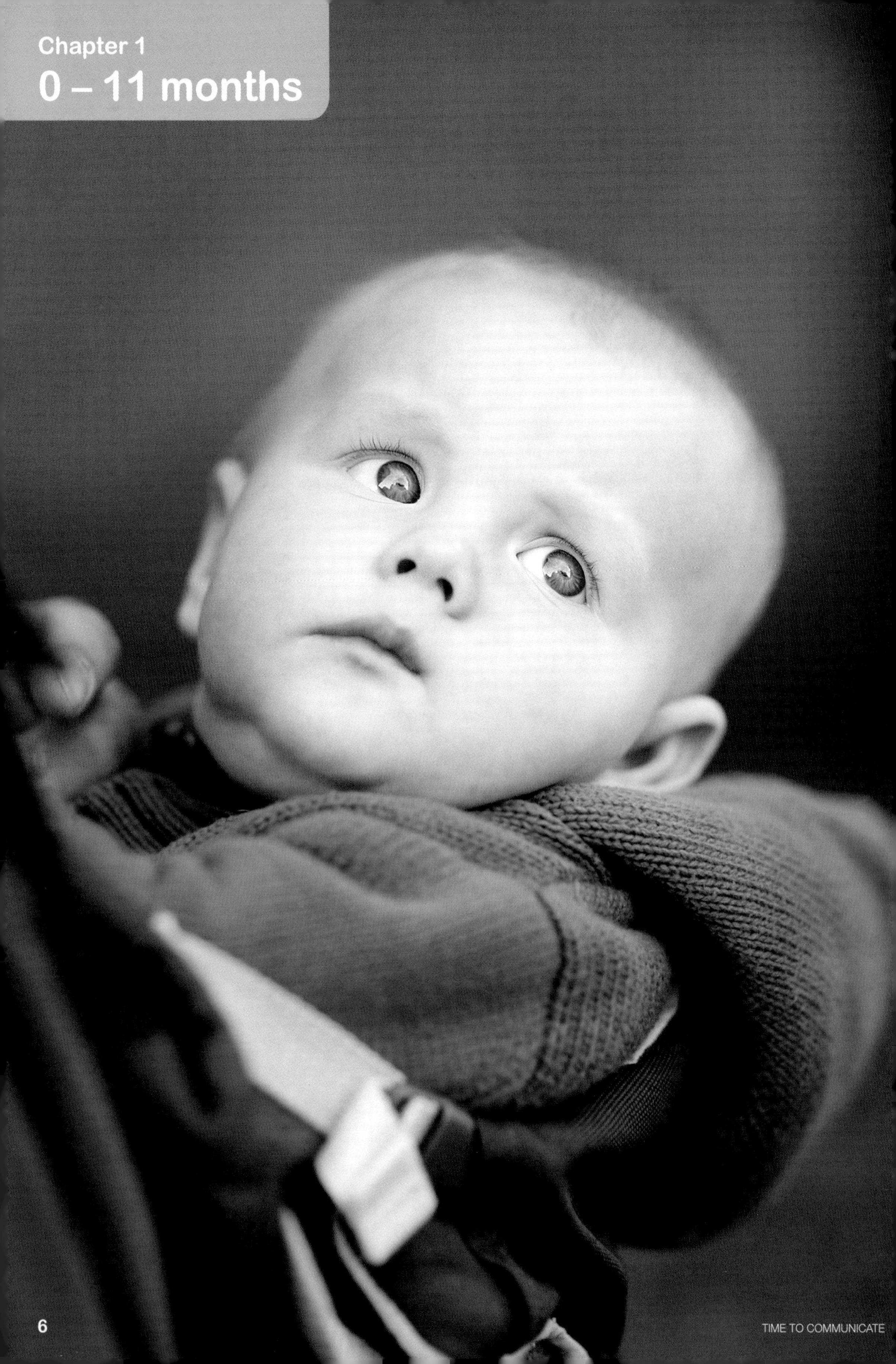

Listening and attention

Early Years Outcomes

Turns towards a familiar sound then locates range of sounds with accuracy.

Listens to, distinguishes and responds to intonations and sounds of voices.

Quietens or alerts to the sound of speech.

Reacts in interaction with others by smiling, looking and moving.

Looks intently at the person talking but stops responding if speaker turns away.

Listens to familiar sounds, words, or finger plays.

***Fleeting attention** – not under child's control, new stimuli takes whole attention.*

Links to the Characteristics of Effective Learning

PLAYING AND EXPLORING

Finding out and exploring

★ showing curiosity about objects, events and people

★ using senses to explore the world around them

e.g. when a practitioner rings sleigh bells near the child, they turn towards the sound.

ACTIVE LEARNING

Being involved and concentrating

★ paying attention to details

*e.g. the child looks closely at an older **sibling** and tries to mimic their smiles.*

Observation	Assessment
What you may notice…	**What it may signify…**

Does the child move their eyes, head or body towards their **prime carer** when they hear their voice?

The child is beginning to locate sounds with a degree of accuracy.

Does the child demonstrate a variety of responses to different voices and **intonation**? E.g. they may be soothed by a calm familiar voice or stimulated by the sound of children's laughter.

The child is beginning to recognise the voices of familiar people and is becoming aware of sounds associated with unknown people.

Does the child often respond with a smile, eye contact or movement when others (usually familiar) attempt to engage with them? Do they focus their attention for as long as that person is speaking?

The child is developing an interest in social interaction and communication with others.

Does the child respond positively to certain familiar sounds, words or finger plays?

The child is starting to recognise familiar sounds and make connections with how these make them feel.

Is the child easily distracted by another noise or movement within their **visual field**?

The child has not yet developed the capacity for **rigid attention**.

Planning
What you can do...

This links to the listening and attention section of the Communication, Language and Literacy Progress Checklist on p27.

Stimulate the child's attention by daily repetition of familiar sounds e.g. face-to-face time with **prime carers**, playing with the same sound making toys, explaining sounds during care routines.

Provide daily opportunities for the child to hear 'conversations' and songs and rhymes that vary in **tone** and liveliness.

Offer periods of sustained eye contact when engaging the child and note if they reciprocate it. Talk directly to the child for short periods throughout the day, especially during care routines.

Use practitioner observations to identify the sounds and songs that interest the child and make sure they are included daily, whilst adding to their **repertoire**.

Introduce short bursts of games such as peek-a-boo and action rhymes to engage the child and start to develop their interest and ability to focus and concentrate.

By 3 months grasping is becoming an intentional response.

By 5 months most children are able to focus on what is happening around them and on objects of interest.

Additional adult-led activities

These are additional activities or guidance to further support this stage of development.

See-saw Margery Daw

See Songs and rhymes on p140 for words and actions.

The Three Blind Mice jiggle

See Songs and rhymes on p137 for words and actions.

Home-time activities

Key communication idea

Strong, positive relationships and secure attachment enable the child's growing brain to become efficient and for their language skills to develop. Make sure time is spent daily fostering this through caring and supportive face-to-face time that meets the child's physical and emotional needs.

Bath time fun

When drying your baby at bath time, wrap them in a towel and sit them on your knee (or lay them on a changing mat) and sing *Bath time I hear thunder*. (See Songs and rhymes on p137 for words and actions.)

By 3 months most children will look at someone speaking to them.

Glossary of terms

Fleeting attention: being able to focus attention for short periods of time. The child is easily distracted and their attention goes to the dominant stimulus in the environment.

Prime carer: the person the child spends most time with e.g. parent at home or key person in a setting.

Intonation: how the voice rises and falls when speaking.

Visual field: the whole area that can be seen by the eye, including that which is seen with side (peripheral) vision.

Rigid attention: the child only focusses on one object or activity. They do not usually look up when their name is called. However, they may shift their attention if they are touched gently as called.

Tone: the pitch, quality, and strength of a musical or vocal sound.

Repertoire: a stock of songs and rhymes that are regularly used.

Understanding

Early Years Outcomes

Stops and looks when hears own name.

Starts to understand contextual clues e.g. familiar gestures, words and sounds.

Links to the Characteristics of Effective Learning

PLAYING AND EXPLORING

Finding out and exploring

★ showing curiosity about objects, events and people

★ using senses to explore the world around them

★ showing particular interests

ACTIVE LEARNING

Being involved and concentrating

★ paying attention to details

E.g. the child hears the creaking sound of the room entry gate as it is opened. They turn their head to look as it might be a familiar adult coming in. The adult smiles and calls the child's name. They wave their arms excitedly as they realise it's their dad.

CREATING AND THINKING CRITICALLY

Making links

★ making links and noticing patterns in their experience

0 – 11 months

Observation **What you may notice...**	Assessment **What it may signify...**
Does the child pause and pay attention when they hear their name?	The child is beginning to understand that a particular name/sound usually relates to them.
Can the child sometimes follow simple instructions such as 'Give me the teddy' (or object they are holding) when accompanied by an outstretched open hand?	The child is beginning to understand some simple words or phrases.
Does the child respond to particular **tones** of voice? E.g. calming to the sound of a soothing voice or lullaby.	The child is starting to understand some contextual clues e.g. a gentle voice is caring and positive, a harsh loud voice is not.

Planning
What you can do...

This links to the understanding section of the Communication, Language and Literacy Progress Checklist on p27.

Use the child's name when engaging with them in play or care routines e.g. when dressing the child say 'Now we put Ali's sock on' pointing to, or gently touching the child as you say their name and showing them the sock as you name it.

Ensure that practitioners are consistent with use of gesture and expression e.g. when saying 'No' they slowly move their head from side to side, keep a straight face and use a calm, low **tone** of voice.

The same applies if the setting uses **Makaton**. All practitioners need to be confident in using the signing regularly throughout the day.

Use observations to reflect on the child's responses to different voices, gestures and words.

During this stage most children recognise their own name.

Additional adult-led activities

These are additional activities or guidance to further support this stage of development.

Naming, labelling and explaining

Help develop a child's understanding by naming and labelling things when you talk about them. Repetition allows the knowledge and understanding to become embedded and stored in the long term memory.

'What's this and what does it do?'

Spend time each day introducing everyday sounds, activities and vocabulary, while also repeating those from previous sessions to develop the child's confidence and understanding.

Soothing songs and action rhymes

Lullabys, soothing songs and action rhymes with contact support the development of communication skills and emotional security e.g. *Tick Tock Hickory Dickory Dock* sung slowly to a steady rhythm, and *1, 2, 3…* (See Songs and rhymes on p141 and p137 for words and actions.)

Home-time activities

Key communication idea

Using gesture alongside speech helps a child to understand what is being said e.g. when praising a child for doing something such as clapping say, 'Well done Safi, good clapping' whilst smiling and clapping yourself.

What are we doing today?

To help develop their understanding, talk to your child and let them know what you're doing whether it's getting them dressed or looking for your car keys. Keep your language simple and name objects as you show them to your child.

Where's Jo? (a peek-a-boo variation)

Engage the child's interest by using their name and smiling at them. Pretend to look around repeatedly saying 'Where's Jo?' then look directly at the child, gently grab their hands or tickle their tummy while smiling and saying 'Here's Jo'.

Glossary of terms

Tone: the pitch, quality, and strength of a musical or vocal sound.

Makaton: a language programme using signs and symbols to help people to communicate. It is designed to support spoken language and the signs and symbols are used with speech, in spoken word order. (See www.makaton.org)

Speaking

Early Years Outcomes

Communicates needs and feelings in a variety of ways including crying, gurgling, babbling and squealing.

Makes own sounds in response when talked to by familiar adults.

Lifts arms in anticipation of being picked up.

Practises and gradually develops speech sounds (babbling) to communicate with adults; says sounds like 'baba, nono, gogo'.

Links to the Characteristics of Effective Learning

PLAYING AND EXPLORING

Finding out and exploring

★ showing curiosity about objects, events and people

★ using senses to explore the world around them

Being willing to 'have a go'

★ initiating activities

CREATING AND THINKING CRITICALLY

Having their own ideas

★ finding new ways to do things

Making links

★ making links and noticing patterns in their experience

e.g. the child 'tries out' a new squealing sound. A practitioner picks them up to see if they are alright and a game of tickle ensues. The child continues to try out the squeal as they have learnt that this is an effective way to gain attention.

ACTIVE LEARNING

Being involved and concentrating

★ maintaining focus on their activity for a period of time

★ showing high levels of energy, fascination

Keep on trying

★ showing a belief that more effort or a different approach will pay off

e.g. when a practitioner who is singing to a child stops to listen to another sound, the baby gurgles and waves their arms to regain attention so that the song continues.

0 – 11 months

Observation
What you may notice...

Assessment
What it may signify...

Does the child make different noises to attract or keep your attention? E.g. squealing in anticipation when you ask, 'Again, again?' whilst wriggling your fingers towards their tummy for a tickle.

The child is becoming aware of gaining a response when using **vocalisation** to express themselves.

Does the child **vocalise** back when spoken to? You may find the child is more responsive when the person is smiling and/or familiar to them.

The child is starting to participate in 'turn-taking' conversations.

Does the child lift their arms to be picked up?

The child is learning to communicate non-verbally in order to gain the response they desire.

Does the child practise cooing and babbling to themselves and with familiar adults when the adult is using **caretaker speech** or **parentese**?

The child is expressing a desire to communicate and is starting to explore the range of sounds they can make both for their own amusement and when communicating with adults.

Planning
What you can do...

This links to the speaking section of the Communication, Language and Literacy Progress Checklist on p27.

Spend time each day responding to, and praising the child's attempts to communicate. Play favourite tickling games such as *I'm coming to hug you* or *Round and round the garden*. (See Songs and rhymes on p138 and p140 for words and actions.)

Engage the child in 'turn-taking' conversations throughout the day by responding positively to the sounds and noises they make. Use your voice playfully to repeat and extend your 'chat'.

Recognise that the child has let you know what they want, e.g. by saying 'Do you want to come out of the cot now? Clever girl, lifting up your arms to let me know!'

*Using **vocalisation** in response and to attract or keep someone's attention is common during this phase.*

Note the types of sounds the child makes and where/when they are most vocal. Use **peer on peer observations** to support colleagues to use their own voices most effectively for this stage.

*Between 6 and 10 months most children are using **reduplicated babble**.*

0 – 11 months

Additional adult-led activities

These are additional activities or guidance to further support this stage of development.

What do I mean?

Children's communication skills develop rapidly during this stage so it is important to share your observations regularly with parents and colleagues so that everyone understands how each child is currently expressing themselves e.g. 'Ca ca ca!' may mean the child has seen the family cat but may also be used when they want a drink!

Story time

Share simple picture books, repeating favourites regularly. Talk about the pictures using simple, short sentences and speak slowly, at about half the usual adult rate. Pay particular attention to anything the child points to or makes noises about or has shown an interest in before, giving them chance to join in with simple sounds.

Every Child a Talker (ECAT)

Make sure you are familiar with these materials available from **www.foundationyears.org.uk**

Home-time activities

Key communication idea

Nappy changing is an ideal time to develop communication and language skills while also forming close attachments during a necessary, regular routine activity. Visit **www.talktoyourbaby@literacytrust.org.uk**

English as an additional language

Speak to parents (or a family member/friend who speaks both languages) and ask them to teach you some key words so that you can support the child's home learning.

Glossary of terms

Vocalise/vocalisation: using the voice to produce sounds or words.

Caretaker speech/parentese: a form of speech often used with babies. It can be higher in **pitch** than usual, has a sing-song quality and is often delivered with a smiling face, wide eyes and head movement.

Peer on peer observation: practitioners observing each other, usually with a specific focus, and giving feedback to support professional development.

Attachments: the affectionate tie between the child and another person.

Reduplicated babbling: repeating the same syllable. For example "baba", "mama".

Reading

Early Years Outcomes

Birth - 11m

Enjoys looking at books and other printed material with familiar people.

8-20m

Handles books and printed material with interest.

16-26m

Interested in books and rhymes and may have favourites.

Links to the Characteristics of Effective Learning

PLAYING AND EXPLORING

Finding out and exploring

★ showing curiosity about objects, events and people

★ using senses to explore the world around them

★ showing particular interests

Being willing to 'have a go'

★ initiating activities

ACTIVE LEARNING

Being involved and concentrating

★ maintaining focus on their activity for a period of time

★ showing high levels of energy, fascination

★ paying attention to details

Keep on trying

★ showing a belief that more effort or a different approach will pay off

e.g. *while sitting in the book area the child picks up a favourite story and puts it in their prime carer's hand who offers to read it and the child settles down in their lap. When the story is finished the **prime carer** puts the book on the shelf. The child picks it up, hands it back saying 'more', and the story is read again.*

Observation	Assessment
What you may notice…	**What it may signify…**

Will the child sit or snuggle with a prime carer or buddy for a short story?

The child enjoys the shared time and is beginning to explore printed materials.

Does the child choose to explore books? (8–20 months).

The child is becoming interested in books and stories.

Can the child recognise favourite characters? Do they attempt to join in favourite rhymes? (16–26 months).

The child is starting to express preferences based on their **recall** of familiar books and rhymes.

Planning
What you can do...

This links to the reading section of the Communication, Language and Literacy Progress Checklist on pages 27, 41 and 55.

Ensure there is a wide range of good quality board, cloth and textured books available for the very young to handle and explore. Make finger puppets to use alongside favourite stories and invent rhymes (such as *Buzzy Bee* or *Butterfly Flutterby* – see p138) to maintain interest and focus. Include these popular books and safe soft toys for the child to play with independently.

Spend time modelling how to hold books, turn pages, lift flaps, press buttons or pull tabs. Display books so that they can be seen and accessed easily from low shelves or baskets. Create cosy, quiet areas for shared book time.

When looking at books and pictures encourage the child to look for and then point to specific objects. Name the object or thing again and encourage the child to repeat the word if they are able. This supports the development of **visual perception**.

Use observations to note popular songs and rhymes and ensure that they are practised and extended into play where possible. For example, if you have been singing *Pat-a-cake* you could encourage the child to sing the rhymes whilst patting and shaping dough to make the cakes, use a plastic or wooden letter to imprint the first letter of their name.

During this stage children may begin to show an interest in and preference for favourite books, songs and rhymes.

Additional adult-led activities

These are additional activities or guidance to further support this stage of development.

Visual perception

It is important to provide regular opportunities to develop **visual perception** and **discrimination** to support future reading skills. For example, posting activities, playing matching games with colours, shapes and sizes (it is the ability to match rather than name that is important). Be aware of potential **colour blindness** when expecting children to identify and match objects by colour alone.

Odd one out

Share simple picture books, repeating favourites regularly. Talk about the pictures using simple, short sentences and speak slowly, at about half the usual adult rate. Pay particular attention to anything the child points to or makes noises about or has shown an interest in before, giving them chance to join in with simple sounds.

Home-time activities

Key communication idea

Looking at books together not only supports a child's language development and future reading skills but also their personal, social and emotional development through strengthening **attachments**.

Wash day fun

Encourage the child to match up clothes as they come out of the washing machine. Find pairs of socks (colour and shape match), same colour clothes, or match by size (daddy's t-shirts are bigger than theirs).

Glossary of terms

Recall: remembering the detail of a previous experience without being prompted.

Visual perception: interpreting and giving meaning to what is seen.

Visual discrimination: distinguishing similarities and differences between shapes and objects.

Colour blindness: an inability to see certain colours (often red, green or blue) in the usual way.

Attachments: the affectionate tie between the child and another person.

Prime carer: the person the child spends most time with e.g. parent at home or key person in a setting.

Early mark making

Laying the foundation stones for later writing development

Early Years Outcomes

Birth - 26m

Children's later writing is based on skills and understandings which they develop as babies and toddlers. Before they can write they need to learn to use spoken language to communicate. Later they learn to write down words they can say.

Early mark making is not the same as writing. It is a sensory and physical experience for babies and toddlers, which they do not yet connect to forming symbols which communicate meaning.

For further information and ideas see 'Time to Move: Physical Development in the Early Years' - *the first book in this series.*

0 – 11 months

Links to the Characteristics of Effective Learning

PLAYING AND EXPLORING

Finding out and exploring

★ showing curiosity about objects, events and people

★ using senses to explore the world around them

★ showing particular interests

Being willing to 'have a go'

★ initiating activities

★ seeking challenge

★ showing a 'can do' attitude

★ taking a risk, engaging in new experiences, and learning by trial and error

CREATING AND THINKING CRITICALLY

Having their own ideas

★ thinking of ideas

★ finding ways to solve problems

★ finding new ways to do things

Making links

★ testing their ideas

Choosing ways to do things

★ changing strategy as needed

ACTIVE LEARNING

Being involved and concentrating

★ maintaining focus on their activity for a period of time

★ showing high levels of energy, fascination

★ not easily distracted

Keep on trying

★ persisting with activity when challenges occur

★ showing a belief that more effort or a different approach will pay off

★ bouncing back after difficulties

Enjoying achieving what they set out to do

★ showing satisfaction in meeting their goals.

*Here is an example of how a child demonstrates the characteristics of effective learning whilst developing their **gross motor skills**. This is a form of sensory and physical development which will lead to greater **fine motor** control. Whilst playing outside a toddler becomes interested in the large tyres which are lying flat on the grass. He looks at them intently, touches them, then climbs into one of them. He spends several minutes inside the tyre, exploring it. He looks across the grass towards his **prime carer**. She waves at him. He climbs out of the tyre and starts to push it towards her. The tyre doesn't move very far so he tries pulling it, still with very little success. His prime carer comes over and asks if he would like some help. He takes her hand and puts it on the tyre. She turns it on its side and shows him how to roll it onto the tarmac. He takes over and rolls the tyre for several minutes, smiling at her from time to time.*

Setting activities

These are activities or guidance to support this stage of development.

Making their mark

For children to become confident and prolific mark makers, practitioners need to provide an emotionally secure environment that values and encourages children's creativity. Provide a wide range of dry and wet materials for the child to explore with their hands and feet. For example, coloured liquids, **gloop**, cold custard, non-allergenic shaving foam, or semolina. Use **commentating** to draw their attention to the marks they are making. For children who may not be comfortable getting their hands or feet covered in paint or other textures, place the material inside a zip-lock bag to allow them to feel and manipulate it without actually touching it.

Finger rhymes

To support **manual dexterity** play finger rhymes. For example, *Two Little Dickie Birds* or *Twinkle Twinkle Little Star.*

Large muscles first

Motor development occurs from the centre outwards. **Gross motor skills**, including **core strength** and shoulder stability need to be well developed before effective **fine motor skills** that are needed for writing can be established. So as well as activities for **manual dexterity** it is essential to provide daily opportunities for children to engage in the physical activities that will support this. These could include crawling, rocking, rolling, spinning, pushing, pulling, and climbing. For example, with a body ball (partially blown up to a soft bouncy level) sit the child on the ball whilst holding their hands and bouncing them gently. As they become more confident let them try and balance. Let them lie on the ball with arms stretched out as you pull and push them gently backwards and forwards.

Home-time activities

Key communication idea

To develop into confident mark makers babies and young children require opportunities and support to experience and explore sensory and tactile materials. Share a range of simple sensory experiences for parents to try at home, for example, cold cooked spaghetti, cold custard or left over pastry to pinch and poke.

Beach baby

If you are lucky enough to live near the sea, spend time on the beach enjoying both wet and dry sand, large pebbles, shells and seaweed. Allow children to dig and build with their hands and feet or a bucket and spade. Alternatively, create a mini beach in a sandpit or baby bath.

Go outdoors

Support the child to safely explore outside. Crawling and rolling on the grass (check it's clear of rubbish and animal mess), climbing steps, low walls and obstacles all help develop a child's **gross motor skills**. Including **muscle resistant play** such as digging, wheeling a child's wheelbarrow and pulling up weeds (under guidance) helps to build muscle strength, body awareness and balance.

Glossary of terms

Gross motor skills: the use of large muscle groups such as those in the arms, legs and core to support a range of physical activities including crawling, rolling, pulling up, sitting and walking.

Gloop: cornflour and water mixed to varying consistencies.

Commentating: speaking out loud about what you notice the child doing whilst you play alongside them. This provides them with new vocabulary and models correct speech.

Manual dexterity: skill in using the hands.

Motor development: the development of muscles and the ability to move around and manipulate the environment.

Core strength: the ability to use tummy and back muscles in a balanced way.

Muscle resistant play: heavy work and proprioceptive play activities that provide resistance so that muscle strength is developed.

Fine motor: movements that require a high degree of control and precision. These may include drawing, writing, cutting with scissors, using cutlery.

Prime carer: the person the child spends most time with e.g. parent at home or key person in a setting.

Progress Checklist: 0 – 11 months: Communication, Language and Literacy

Name ....

Date						
Age in months						

Use different coloured pens to track assessments so that progress can be seen.
Tick 'yes' if the child consistently demonstrates this. Tick 'some difficulty' if the child can sometimes demonstrate this.
Tick 'severe difficulty' if the child rarely or never demonstrates this.

	Yes	Some difficulty	Severe difficulty
Listening and attention			
The child moves their eyes, head or body towards their prime carer when they hear their voice.			
The child demonstrates a variety of responses to different voices and **intonation** e.g. they may be soothed by a calm familiar voice or stimulated by the sound of children's laughter.			
The child often responds with a smile, eye contact or movement when others (usually familiar) attempt to engage them. They focus their attention for as long as that person is speaking.			
The child responds positively to certain familiar sounds, words or finger plays – note which ones.			
The child is easily distracted by another noise or movement within their **visual field.**			
Understanding			
Does the child pause and pay attention when they hear their name?			
Can the child sometimes follow simple instructions such as 'Give me the teddy' (or object they are holding) when accompanied by an outstretched open hand?			
Does the child respond to particular **tones** of voice? E.g. calming to the sound of a soothing voice or lullaby.			
Speaking			
Does the child make different noises to attract or keep your attention? For example, squealing in anticipation when you ask 'Again, again?' whilst wriggling your fingers towards their tummy for a tickle. Note significant responses and meanings.			
Does the child **vocalise** back when spoken to? You may find the child is more responsive when the person is smiling and/or familiar to them.			
Does the child lift their arms to be picked up?			
Does the child practise cooing and babbling to themselves and with familiar adults when the adult is using **caretaker speech** or **parentese**?			
Reading			
Will the child sit or snuggle with a **prime carer** or buddy for a short story?			
Writing			
There are no specific outcomes for this stage of development. You may wish to refer to progress checklist 0-11 months in *Time to Move*, which is linked to the physical development needed for later writing.			

Time to Communicate © Trudi Fitzhenry and Karen Murphy, published by Featherstone 2015

Listening and attention

Early Years Outcomes

Moves whole body to sounds they enjoy, such as music or a regular beat.

Has a strong exploratory impulse.

Concentrates intently on an object or activity of own choosing for short periods.

Pays attention to dominant stimulus – easily distracted by noises or other people talking.

Links to the Characteristics of Effective Learning

PLAYING AND EXPLORING

Finding out and exploring

★ showing curiosity about objects, events and people

★ using senses to explore the world around them

★ engaging in open-ended activity

★ showing particular interests

Being willing to 'have a go'

★ initiating activities

e.g. when the child hears a particular song or piece of music, they move enthusiastically by waving their arms and legs or bouncing their whole body.

ACTIVE LEARNING

Being involved and concentrating

★ maintaining focus on their activity for a period of time

★ showing high levels of energy, fascination

★ paying attention to details

e.g. when exploring the contents of the kitchen cupboard or a treasure basket, the child is first attracted by the sounds each object makes as they are pulled out. They then explore the objects in turn, following the adult's lead.

8 – 20 months

Observation	Assessment
What you may notice...	**What it may signify...**

Does the child bounce their knees, sway their body or move their arms to familiar songs or rhymes?

The child is beginning to express a preference for types of songs, rhymes or music. They are starting to develop their sense of **rhythm** and **beat**.

Does the child enjoy trying out new activities? Is their attention drawn to new sounds and people?

The child is curious about their environment and confident to engage with new experiences.

Can the child maintain their focus on objects and activities of interest for between 1 and 3 minutes?

The child's **concentration span** is increasing. If the child does not focus on the activity they may not be sufficiently interested in the activities and resources offered.

Is the child easily distracted from their play by other voices or sounds?

The child may not yet have developed the capacity for **rigid attention**.

Planning
What you can do...

This links to the listening and attention section of the Communication, Language and Literacy Progress checklist on p41.

Provide daily opportunities for moving and singing along to action songs and rhymes with a strong steady beat e.g. *Shakey, shakey* (See Songs and rhymes on p140 for words and actions.)

Closely observe children's reactions to new activities, people and sounds. For those who engage eagerly, provide regular opportunities to explore new resources and activities freely. For those who are more tentative, ensure that a **prime carer** is available to model new resources and give emotional support and confidence to try new things.

Ensure that resources and activities available are monitored regularly, not only for safety and cleanliness but also usage. Use individual observations to assess which resources and activities best engage each child and support the next steps in their learning.

By 9 months most children are interested in and watch the activities of others.

Where possible try to provide quiet, possibly enclosed spaces for children to play. Audit the play environment and look for ways of increasing **sound absorption**.

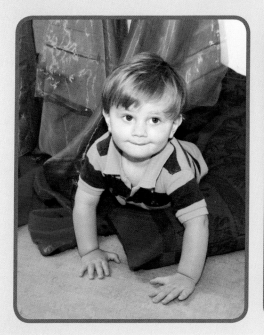

Additional adult-led activities

These are additional activities or guidance to further support this stage of development.

Too many sounds

In the beginning phases of learning to listen, good **acoustic** conditions are essential. Children at this stage of development are not able to filter out background or additional noise to the same degree that adults can. Any noise may be a distraction that will make learning to listen harder. Adults' spoken language should be clear and children should have daily opportunities to play in a quiet listening environment.

Communication friendly spaces

Think about how you can create quiet yet stimulating spaces, both indoors and outside, that encouage both listening and speaking e.g. a pop-up tent with cosy cushions and sound toys that children can crawl or toddle into.

Home-time activities

Key communication idea

When singing songs and rhymes with your child choose ones that involve actions and movement (see Songs and rhymes on p137 for words and actions) so that they can feel really involved. (Initially you will need to model the actions and help your child to join in). Repeating favourite songs and rhymes is essential to develop their listening and spoken skills.

Baby *Grand Old Duke of York*

See Songs and rhymes on p137 for words and actions.

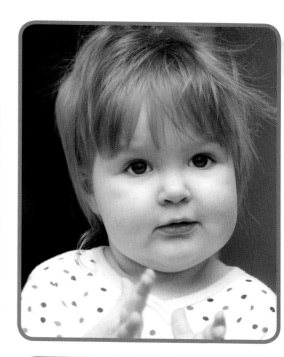

Glossary of terms

Rhythm: a repeated pattern of movement or sound, or a steady beat.

Beat: the pulse (regularly repeating event).

Prime carer: the person the child spends most time with e.g. parent at home or key person in a setting.

Concentration span: the length of time a person, or group, is able to concentrate on something or remain interested.

Rigid attention: the child only focuses on one object or activity. They do not usually look up when their name is called. However, they may shift their attention if they are touched gently as called.

Sound absorption: the degree of sound absorbed by materials. Soft furnishings such as drapes, rugs, and cushions absorb more sound than harder reflective surfaces such as tiled floors, tables or windows.

Acoustic: the properties or qualities of a room or building that determine how sound is transmitted in it.

Understanding

Early Years Outcomes

Developing the ability to follow others' body language, including pointing and gesture.

Responds to the different things said when in a familiar context with a special person (e.g. 'Where's Mummy?', 'Where's your nose?').

Understanding of single words in context is developing, e.g. 'cup', 'milk', 'daddy'.

Links to the Characteristics of Effective Learning

PLAYING AND EXPLORING

Finding out and exploring

★ showing curiosity about objects, events and people

★ using senses to explore the world around them

★ showing particular interests

e.g. the child seems interested in another child's water bottle. You support their curiosity, letting them hold and look at the bottle but as they attempt to put it towards their mouth you substitute it for their own bottle and explain simply and calmly that this is their bottle.

CREATING AND THINKING CRITICALLY

Making links

★ making links and noticing patterns in their experience

e.g. when you call the child's name and point to the big board book you are holding, they look – then crawl towards you. You reward them with a smile and the story.

ACTIVE LEARNING

Being involved and concentrating

★ paying attention to details

e.g. while you are naming the objects in one of the treasure baskets and showing them to the child they start to pay particular attention to some feathers. They remain interested as you blow the feathers, attempting to blow them for themselves.

Observation
What you may notice...

Assessment
What it may signify...

Does the child watch as you point to objects and people?

The child is becoming aware that you are communicating something to them and is interested **(joint attention)**.

Can the child point to or find favourite familiar people or objects when asked?

The child is able to demonstrate understanding of a simple instruction.

Does the child show recognition of some single words in context? E.g. when offering a toy, the practitioner says 'car?'; the child looks, accepts the toy, and plays or looks away rejecting it.

The child is beginning to understand some words that are important to them.

Planning
What you can do...

This links to the understanding section of the Communication, Language and Literacy Progress Checklist on p41.

Whenever you point to something or hold something out to the child keep your language simple. E.g. 'Ahmed, look at the basket of shells.' Once their attention is gained, offer the basket to the child and allow them to explore.

Praise the child with smiles, hand claps and a light happy voice whenever they successfully respond to a request.

Repeatedly name and label people and objects that have the child's attention to develop their understanding and link the word to its meaning.

At around 12 months most children are able to index-finger point to direct other's attention.

Additional adult-led activities

These are additional activities or guidance to further support this stage of development.

What's coming next?

Children anticipate actions such as tickles, actions and loud or strange noises in familiar rhymes and songs so use these throughout the day to consolidate their learning. Help them to do the actions if they want to join in but aren't quite able to do so without support. Add new songs to maintain interest and build vocabulary e.g. *Ten Galloping Horses; Slowly, Slowly, Very Slowly; Hickory Dickory Dock*. (See Songs and rhymes on p141 and p141).

What's it for?

Encourage **functional use** of objects after plenty of opportunities to explore by repeatedly demonstrating/modelling/labelling and encouraging with smiling, eye contact and by using an expressive voice.

Home-time activities

Key communication idea

At this stage of development children are beginning to associate meaning to many of the environmental sounds around them, e.g. a telephone ringing or a car pulling onto the drive. Parents can support this learning by identifying, naming and explaining simply what has attracted the child's attention.

What's this?

Once the child is familiar with a variety of sounds collect two objects such as a bunch of keys and a mobile phone. Show them to the child whilst making the sound and naming the object then hide them in a shopping bag. Make the noise and ask 'What's that noise?' Make the noise again. If they have some language, let them attempt to tell you or ask 'Is it mummy's keys?' When the child nods or says yes, pull them out of the bag and praise them. If they enjoy the game and find it easy add more objects.

Glossary of terms

Joint attention: the shared focus of two individuals on an object or person.

Functional use: using objects for the purpose they were designed for.

Speaking

Early Years Outcomes

Uses sounds in play, e.g. 'brrrm' for toy car.

Uses single words.

Frequently imitates words and sounds.

Enjoys babbling and increasingly experiments with using sounds and words to communicate for a range of purposes (e.g. teddy, more, no, bye-bye).

Uses pointing with eye gaze to make requests, and to share an interest.

Creates personal words as they begin to develop language.

Links to the Characteristics of Effective Learning

PLAYING AND EXPLORING

Finding out and exploring

★ showing curiosity about objects, events and people

★ engaging in open ended activity

★ showing particular interests

Playing with what they know

★ representing their experiences in play

e.g. on a visit to the local farm the child is fascinated by the sheep. They watch the lambs being fed and look between the lamb and the ewe. The practitioner notices this and crouches down to name the animals and the sound they make. The child copies the 'baa' sound.

ACTIVE LEARNING

Being involved and concentrating

★ maintaining focus on their activity for a period of time

★ showing high levels of energy, fascination

★ paying attention to details

Enjoying achieving what they set out to do

★ enjoying meeting challenges for their own sake rather than external awards or praise

CREATING AND THINKING CRITICALLY

Having their own ideas

★ finding new ways to do things

Making links

★ making links and noticing patterns in their experience

e.g. on returning to the setting the child chooses to play with the model farm. They move the sheep around the floor and make a 'baa' sound. The practitioner plays alongside the child and talks about the other animals, making their corresponding sounds. The child listens as they play with the sheep.

Observation
What you may notice...

Assessment
What it may signify...

Observation	Assessment
Can the child imitate some animal or vehicle sounds in play?	The child is starting to connect the sounds that familiar things make with sounds they can create themselves.
Is the child starting to use some recognisable words, often with the end sounds missed off such as 'baba' for bye bye or 'dada' for daddy? Does the child join in a "conversation" with you, attempting to copy the words or sounds you use?	The child is beginning to understand that words and sounds convey meaning in familiar situations. Their **situational understanding** is developing. The child is becoming more confident at using language to express themselves and their needs or interests.
Does the child appear content to babble to themselves when concentrating intently on an object? Do they babble to a familiar adult in an attempt to express an interest or need?	The child is exploring the range of sounds they can make and is beginning to use more recognisable words when they communicate with others.
Does the child look at an object or person then back to you to draw your attention to it?	The child is using **eye pointing** to make their intentions clear.
Does the child use words that sound like their meaning, or make up words to represent a sound they aren't able to enunciate clearly yet? E.g. a little girl called Rosie may refer to herself as 'Woddy'.	The child is using their own interpretation of sounds and words they hear in order to communicate.

Planning
What you can do...

This links to the speaking section of the Communication, Language and Literacy Progress Checklist on p41.

Play alongside the child, imitating their sounds before extending the language and introducing more sounds e.g. they are 'brrrming' as they push a car along. You do the same with a fire engine adding 'nee-naah, nee-naah, fire engine here'.

Repeat words back so that the child hears it spoken clearly and correctly. If the child is referring to an object or person, pick it up or point to it/them to show that you understand and value their efforts.

By 16 months most children are saying their first words

Encourage the child to use and explore their own voice by drawing their attention to the sounds around them and by using your voice playfully, varying **pitch** and **volume** in games such as tube talk. Attract the child's attention by calling their name through a tube, into their tube. If they are already using some **vocalisation** say these words or sounds into the tube, for example 'doggie woof'!

Encourage all vocal attempts at interaction by responding positively and in a playful, friendly voice or using **caretaker speech**. Provide muscle strengthening activities such as blowing toy windmills, musical instruments like trumpets, wooden train whistles and drinking through a straw (especially thicker liquids like smoothies).

Observe the child carefully so that you don't miss any opportunities to respond positively to their attempts at communication. Once they have your attention engage them in conversation, and where possible meet their need e.g. the child looks up at a toy that is just out of reach, then at you, then back to the toy. Ask them if they want the toy, name it, and then pass it to them and engage in play. This will build their growing vocabulary.

Pay particular attention to all vocal communication. Note any discoveries and share them with all practitioners that work with the child to minimise possible frustration if they don't understand what the child is attempting to say. Keeping a 'chatter matters' diary can support this shared understanding of a child's developing speech.

Additional adult-led activities

These are additional activities or guidance to further support this stage of development.

Face to face

Speaking slowly and **enunciating** clearly whilst facing the child gives them the opportunity to observe your expressions and see the shape of your mouth when talking.

Home-time activities

Key communication idea

As the child begins to experiment with sounds and words they need praise and encouragement. Playing a simple game with two known objects can support the child's developing vocabulary and also increase their understanding of **information carrying words**. Put two familiar objects on the floor near the child (e.g. a ball and a cup). Say, 'Give me the cup' but do not point out the cup in anyway. If the child identifies the cup and passes it to you, praise them! Demonstrating how this game works first will help your child to understand how to play. 'Give me' can be replaced with other commands e.g. 'Show me' or "Find me'.

Home words

Talk to parents about how their child uses language/words at home so that you can support them in your setting e.g. 'noo-noo' might be a special word that means their comfort blanket that they have in their bag for sleep/rest times. Also share any new sounds/ words being heard in your setting.

The Early Years Outcomes for Reading are combined in the EYFS for ages 0 – 26 months.

Reading 8-20m refer to Chapter 1 pages 19-22.

For Writing 8-20m refer to Chapter 1 pages 23-26.

Background music

Young children are not able to filter out background noises (TV, radio etc.) as effectively as adults, and need to be able to hear new vocabulary and speech sounds clearly to **assimilate** them. It is important to use background music selectively and for a purpose e.g. playing soothing music to aid sleep or rest.

Glossary of terms

Situational understanding: when words are recognized in everyday situations e.g. 'bed' at bed time.

Eye pointing: using the eyes to communicate.

Pitch: how high or low a musical note or sound is.

Volume: how loud or quiet a musical note or sound is.

Vocalise/vocalisation: using the voice to produce sounds or words.

Assimilate: to take in and understand.

Enunciate: say or pronounce words or sounds.

Information carrying words: a word that carries meaning e.g. Where's the cat? In this question, *cat* is the information carrying word. A child shows their understanding of the meaning if they can identify the cat amongst other objects without being given any clues (pointing or gesturing towards the cat).

Progress Checklist: 8 – 20 months: Communication, Language and Literacy

Name ....

Date						
Age in months						

Use different coloured pens to track assessments so that progress can be seen.
Tick 'yes' if the child consistently demonstrates this. Tick 'some difficulty' if the child can sometimes demonstrate this.
Tick 'severe difficulty' if the child rarely or never demonstrates this.

	Yes	Some difficulty	Severe difficulty
Listening and attention			
Does the child bounce their knees, sway their body or move their arms to familiar songs or rhymes? Note any particularly popular ones.			
Does the child enjoy trying out new activities?			
Is their attention drawn to new sounds and people?			
Can the child maintain their focus on objects and activities of interest for between 1 and 3 minutes? Note how long and which activities.			
Is the child easily distracted from their play by other voices or sounds?			
Understanding			
Does the child watch as you point to objects and people?			
Can the child point to or find favourite familiar people or objects when asked? Note who, and which objects.			
Does the child show recognition of some single words in context? For example, when offering a toy, the practitioner says 'Car?' and the child looks, accepts the toy and plays or looks away rejecting it.			
Speaking			
Can the child imitate some animal or vehicle sounds in play? Note which ones.			
Is the child starting to use some recognisable words, often with the end sounds missed off (such as 'baba' for 'bye bye' or 'dada' for 'daddy'). Note which ones.			
Does the child join in a "conversation" with you, attempting to copy the words or sounds you use?			
Does the child appear content to babble to themselves when concentrating intently on an object?			
Do they babble to a familiar adult in an attempt to express an interest or need?			
Does the child look at an object or person then back to you to draw your attention to it?			
Does the child use words that sound like their meaning or make up words to represent a sound they aren't able to enunciate clearly yet? For example; a little girl called Rosie may refer to herself as 'Woddy'. Note any and their meaning.			
Reading			
Does the child choose to explore books? Note any favourites.			
Writing			
There are no specific outcomes for this stage of development. You may wish to refer to progress checklist 8-20 months in *Time to Move* which is linked to the physical development needed for later writing.			

Time to Communicate © Trudi Fitzhenry and Karen Murphy, published by Featherstone 2015

Listening and attention

Early Years Outcomes

Listens to and enjoys rhythmic patterns in rhymes and stories.

Enjoys rhymes and demonstrates listening by trying to join in with actions or vocalisations.

***Rigid attention** – may appear not to hear.*

Links to the Characteristics of Effective Learning

PLAYING AND EXPLORING

Finding out and exploring

★ using senses to explore the world around them

★ engaging in open-ended activity

★ showing particular interests

Being willing to 'have a go'

★ initiating activities

★ showing a 'can do' attitude

e.g. when playing with toys in the 'vet's corner', the child opens a box and sees a cuddly lion inside. They laugh and say 'too fierce!' and roar. The practitioner follows the child's cue and reads 'Dear Zoo' with the child.

ACTIVE LEARNING

Being involved and concentrating

★ maintaining focus on their activity for a period of time

★ showing high levels of energy, fascination

★ not easily distracted

★ paying attention to details

Enjoying achieving what they set out to do

★ showing satisfaction in meeting their own goals

e.g. having watched other children take part in a familiar song or rhyme, the child attempts to repeat simple actions and phrases. The child claps their hands and smiles when the practitioner praises them for joining in.

16 – 26 months

Observation
What you may notice...

Assessment
What it may signify...

Does the child listen to rhymes and stories and ask for the same ones again and again? Do they clap along or move their body rhythmically even if they are not quite ready to do the appropriate actions?

The child is developing an interest in sound and rhythm, and is beginning to respond physically.

Does the child join in with parts of their favourite songs or rhymes? Do you sometimes hear snippets of songs and rhymes while the child is playing?

The child is beginning to remember and can **recall** at will some favourite phrases or rhymes.

Can the child stop and look at an adult when their name is called and then continue with the activity?

The child is developing **single channelled attention**.

Does the child continue with an activity and not respond when you call their name or use a setting signal for children to listen?

The child may be operating at the **rigid attention** stage.

At this stage of development, most children listen to speech directed to them.

Planning
What you can do...

This links to the listening and attention section of the Communication, Language and Literacy Progress Checklist on p55.

Provide daily opportunities for singing and rhyming, both in small groups and alongside play. Choose rhyming stories that include lift the flap activities or make up your own (just remember if it's popular you'll need to be able to repeat it!).

Ensure children can practise the songs and rhymes they like. Play *What's in the box?*, making sure the objects relate to the child's interests. (See Songs and rhymes p141 for song and actions).

If the child is developing the ability to shift their attention it is important to praise them whenever they stop doing something they are enjoying, to listen to you. Try to give them opportunities to return to their chosen activity, either immediately or later in the day. Make sure you explain clearly when this will be possible.

For those children who have reached the **rigid attention** stage try to attract their attention by gently touching their arms or shoulder.

By 2 years most children can relate two named objects for example 'Put the blocks on the table'.

At around 18 months many children will attempt to sing or join in with favourite songs or rhymes.

When a child responds to your request for their attention give them lots of warm praise!

Additional adult-led activities

These are additional activities or guidance to further support this stage of development.

Daily dose

For children to acquire good listening and speaking skills they need regular, fun, multi-sensory input from sensitive adults. *Letters and Sounds: Phase One (DfES)* provides activities to support a broad and rich language experience.

Who has…?

This game is played in pairs or a small group. You need a selection of rhyming objects e.g. a car and a star, a dog and a frog. The adult keeps one of each rhyming pair and lets the child/ren choose one each from the pairs. The adult says 'I have got a star. Who has got my car?' Encourage the child with the car to hold it up and everybody says 'Sahil has got the car'. Put the star and the car together and repeat: 'A star and a car, thank-you Sahil'. Continue until everyone has had a go or interest wanes.

Home-time activities

Key communication idea

Developing your child's listening and attention skills at home through games and rhymes helps to prepare them for the later skills of reading and writing. Share some laminated copies of popular nursery rhymes and simple rhyming games for parents to borrow.

Rhyme time

Consider making rhyme time story sacks containing a CD (with an actions card) of the rhymes you sing in your setting. For parents for whom English is an additional language create picture/photo cards to explain the actions.

Glossary of terms

Recall: remembering the detail of a previous experience without being prompted.

Rigid attention: the child only focuses on one object or activity. They do not usually look up when their name is called. However, they may shift their attention if they are touched gently when called.

Single channelled attention: the child can shift attention, for example from a task to an instruction then back, as long as their full attention is gained. Touching the child gently on the arm or shoulder may help.

Understanding

Early Years Outcomes

Selects familiar objects by name and will go and find objects when asked, or identify objects from a group.

Understands simple sentences (e.g. 'Throw the ball.')

Links to the Characteristics of Effective Learning

PLAYING AND EXPLORING

Finding out and exploring

★ showing curiosity about objects, events and people

★ using senses to explore the world around them

★ showing particular interests

e.g. the child enjoys hide-and-seek games, particularly if they involve digging for treasure in the outdoor area.

ACTIVE LEARNING

Being involved and concentrating

★ maintaining focus on their activity for a period of time

★ not easily distracted

★ paying attention to details

e.g. you ask the child to wash their hands for snack time. They are able to go to the sink, walking past a number of interesting activities and some friends, wash their hands and return ready to select some fruit and a drink.

Observation
What you may notice...

Can the child point to or pick out a familiar object from a group? Can they go and find things on request?

Is the child starting to name favourite toys, objects and people? They may use approximate forms of words such as 'goggy' for dog.

Can the child respond to simple instructions such as 'Get your coat', and 'Put the train on the track'?

Assessment
What it may signify...

The child is developing their receptive vocabulary which enables them to recognise more everyday objects by their names and without seeing them.

The child can understand and follow simple instructions.

Planning
What you can do...

This links to the understanding section of the Communication, Language and Literacy Progress Checklist on p55.

Play simple hide-and-seek games e.g. take two or three familiar objects and bury them in the sand tray while the child is looking. Name them as you hide them, then ask 'where's the dog?', while gesturing with open hands. Encourage the child to dig in the sand and find it, helping if necessary. Then praise the child and name the object again when found. Extend the game by including hiding objects in separate locations around the room and outside.

Play games that involve simple instructions e.g. *What have I done with my shoe today?* to the tune of *Here we go round the mulberry bush*. Identify vocabulary you wish to introduce or embed. Select relevant objects (two of each). 'Hide' one in plain sight nearby, place the other in front of the children. Sing:

What have I done with my shoe today, shoe today, shoe today?

What have I done with my shoe today?

Can Jay see?

The name 'Jay' can be substituted for any child's name. Ask Jay to find the hidden shoe. Repeat until everyone has had at least one go.

Up to 2 years of age, 's' is not always used when saying words, e.g. 'tea-tide' is said to mean 'sea-side'.

During this stage most children are able to follow simple instructions such as 'Find me a ball.'

By 24 months some children can put two or three short words together in a sentence, for example 'Look! I got it!'

Additional adult-led activities

These are additional activities or guidance to further support this stage of development.

Key communication idea

The development of children's understanding of communication and language relies on both **cognitive development** and social skills. Practitioners need to model good, clear quality language and make meaning **explicit** whenever interacting with children.

Small world play

Select a small world person or animal and play alongside children **commentating** as you play to increase the child's **receptive vocabulary** and understanding of sentence structure.

Find me, name me

In a small group of two or three, ask children to choose three small, portable objects in the room or outside area to photograph with you. Print out the photos (you may wish to laminate them and use again!), name and discuss where the object was or is now. Shuffle the photos and ask the children to take turns to select one then find the object and bring it to you, naming it if possible.

Home-time activities

Key communication idea

Remember to keep your language simple e.g. give one instruction such as, 'Come to Mummy' whilst holding out your arms or hand. Speak slowly and clearly, repeating new words and explaining your actions e.g. 'Nana's putting the baked beans away. In the cupboard go the baked beans.'

What's this?

Support your child's developing understanding by playing this game. Label a facial feature or body part and add a sound e.g. 'Daddy's nose, beep, beep.' (Touch your own nose.) 'Ranil's nose, beep, beep.' (Touch your child's nose.) Repeat the words, encouraging your child to perform the actions for themselves, make the sounds – and possibly attempt to label the body part.

Glossary of terms

Receptive vocabulary: the bank of words a child recognises and understands.

Cognitive development: the ability to think and understand.

Explicit: clear and easily understood.

Commentating: using language alongside a child to describe what you or they are doing or seeing.

Speaking

Early Years Outcomes

Copies familiar expressions e.g. 'Oh dear', 'All gone'.

Beginning to put two words together e.g. 'want ball', 'more juice'.

Uses different types of everyday words (nouns, verbs and adjectives) e.g. banana, go, sleep, hot).

Beginning to ask simple questions.

Beginning to talk about people and things that are not present.

Links to the Characteristics of Effective Learning

PLAYING AND EXPLORING

Finding out and exploring

★ showing curiosity about objects, events and people

★ using senses to explore the world around them

★ showing particular interests

Being willing to 'have a go'

★ initiating activities

CREATING AND THINKING CRITICALLY

Having their own ideas

★ finding ways to solve problems

*e.g. Albin spends 10 minutes with his **prime carer** playing with a pop up toy. He says 'wat dat?' each time he tries to push, turn or slide a button. His prime carer explains and helps him using simple language for each action which Albin tries to copy.*

ACTIVE LEARNING

Being involved and concentrating

★ maintaining focus on their activity for a period of time

★ showing high levels of energy and fascination

Observation
What you may notice...

Assessment
What it may signify...

Is the child able to wait and join in with 'ready, steady, go!' when playing running and chasing games outside?

▷ The child is beginning to link the words or phrase with an action or meaning.

Can the child use some two word phrases such as 'Mummy gone'?

▷ The child is attempting to express what they notice, or a need or desire through speech.

Does the child use a range of everyday words to name and describe familiar objects, actions and events?

▷ The child's **receptive vocabulary** and **recall** of familiar words is continuing to grow in line with their stage of development.

Does the child use **inflection** to ask simple questions e.g. 'Billy home?'

▷ The child is copying the **inflection** they hear when adults ask questions.

Does the child talk about family members or favourite toys while in the setting?

▷ The child has developed an understanding of **object permanence**.

Planning
What you can do...

This links to the speaking section of the Communication, Language and Literature Progress Checklist on p55.

Continue to provide regular opportunities for the child to hear and practise familiar expressions. Share with colleagues the words or phrases you would like to focus on for that day or week. Read familiar stories that contain plenty of repetition.

Support the child's understanding of how sentences work by modelling and expanding e.g. the child says 'fall down' as the bricks they are stacking tumble. You say, 'The bricks have fallen down'. Remember to be careful not to expand too much or the child will not make the connection.

Take every opportunity to expand a child's **repertoire** by **commentating** during playful activities e.g. while outside playing in puddles, say: 'We're splish, splosh, splashing in the puddles'. Include in your planning specific vocabulary or sentence structures that you wish to focus on e.g. 'My turn', 'Your turn', 'Antonio's turn'.

Respond positively to questions even if you have heard the same one many times, as children often use them to gain reassurance. Encourage children's thinking and speaking by asking and encouraging **open-ended questions**. Remember to allow plenty of time for the child to think then respond.

Encourage the child to talk about people and favourite objects (possibly **transitional objects**). Be aware that they may do so because they are missing the person or object, and need your support and reassurance that they will see the person or object again and that they or it are safe.

By the end of this developmental stage many children will be able to use most vowel sounds and the letters m,p,b,n,t, and w in their speech.

Children at this stage may use approximate forms of words. For example 'goggy' for 'dog'.

Additional adult-led activities

These are additional activities or guidance to further support this stage of development.

Daily dose

Make time to have at least one conversation every session that the child attends. Make sure you're at the child's level and that you have their attention before you start. Remember to use statements rather than lots of direct questions, as these can make the child feel that they are being quizzed and that there are right and wrong answers. It may be appropriate to use and support **augmentive methods of communication**.

Home-time activities

Key communication idea

It is important that children at this stage of development are given regular opportunities to continue to build their vocabulary throughout the day. Wherever possible give simple choices involving two items, naming them clearly and giving the child the chance to make their choice through gesture or speech. If the child attempts a word or says it incorrectly, do not correct them but acknowledge their choice by repeating the word back correctly e.g. the child says 'zuma' for 'satsuma', and the adult replies 'Do you want the satsuma?'

Bubbles and butterflies

To strengthen the child's mouth muscles and support the pronunciation of words, try bubble blowing. Use a large wand and tray, or at bath time put a handful of bubbles onto their hands for them to blow them away. You could also cut out butterfly shapes from thin tissue paper, put one onto the child's hand and get them to make the butterfly fly.

The Early Years Outcomes for Reading are combined in the EYFS for ages 0 – 26 months.

For Reading 16-26m refer to chapter 1 pages 19-22.

For Writing 16-20m refer to chapter 1 pages 23-26.

My favourite things

Create a display or book for children to bring in pictures or a token reminder of their favourite people and things from family and at home to encourage them to talk about them when they are not there.

EAL

Remember to acknowledge and praise all attempts at communication even if you don't understand the actual words and are unable to repeat them. Respond in English, speaking slowly, clearly and without using too many words. Speak to parents for clarification on words or phrases the child is using so that you are able to understand their needs and show the child that you value their efforts.

Glossary of terms

Receptive vocabulary: the bank of words a child recognises and understands.

Recall: remembering the detail of a previous experience without being prompted.

Inflection: the rise or fall in the voice for emphasis e.g. the voice often rises towards the end of a word or sentence to indicate that it is a question.

Object permanence: understanding that things continue to exist even when they cannot be seen, heard, touched, smelt or sensed.

Repertoire: a stock of words, songs and rhymes that are regularly used.

Commentating: speaking out loud about what you notice the child doing whilst you play alongside them. This provides them with new vocabulary and models correct speech.

Transitional object: a familiar object used to provide psychological comfort for small children.

Open-ended questions: questions that can't be answered with one or two words. They generally require more thoughtful responses. Open-ended questions usually begin with who, why, what or how.

Augmentive methods of communication: alternative ways of communicating such as Makaton, British Sign language (BSL) or electronic aids.

Progress Checklist: 16 – 26 months: Communication, Language and Literacy

Name ....

Date						
Age in months						

Use different coloured pens to track assessments so that progress can be seen.
Tick 'yes' if the child consistently demonstrates this. Tick 'some difficulty' if the child can sometimes demonstrate this.
Tick 'severe difficulty' if the child rarely or never demonstrates this.

	Yes	Some difficulty	Severe difficulty
Listening and attention			
Does the child listen to rhymes and stories and ask for the same ones again and again? Note favourites.			
Do they clap along or move their body rhythmically even if they are not quite ready to do the appropriate actions?			
Does the child join in with parts of their favourite songs or rhymes? Note which ones.			
Do you sometimes hear snippets of songs and rhymes while the child is playing? Note which ones.			
Can the child stop and look at an adult when their name is called, then continue with the activity?			
Does the child continue with an activity and not respond when you call their name?			
Does the child continue with an activity and not respond when you use a setting signal for children to listen?			
Understanding			
Can the child point to or pick out a familiar object from a group? Can they go and find things on request?			
Is the child starting to name favourite toys, objects and people? They may use approximate forms of words such as 'goggy' for 'dog'. Note words and meanings.			
Can the child carry out simple instructions such as 'Get your coat?' and 'Put the train on the track'?			
Speaking			
Is the child able to wait and joins in with 'ready, steady, go!' when playing running and chasing games outside?			
Can the child use some two word phrases such as 'mummy gone'? Note phrases.			
Does the child use a range of everyday words to name and describe familiar objects, actions and events?			
Does the child use **inflection** to ask simple questions. For example, 'Billy home?'			
Does the child talk about family members or favourite toys while in the setting?			
Reading			
Can the child recognise favourite characters?			
Do they attempt to join in favourite rhymes? Note which ones.			
Writing			
There are no specific outcomes for this stage of development. You may wish to refer to progress checklist 8-20 months in *Time to Move* which is linked to the physical development needed for later writing.			

Time to Communicate © Trudi Fitzhenry and Karen Murphy, published by Featherstone 2015

TIME TO COMMUNICATE

Listening and attention

Early Years Outcomes

Listens with interest to the noises adults make when they read stories.

Recognises and responds to many familiar sounds e.g. turning to a knock on the door, looking at or going to the door.

Shows interest in play with sounds, songs and rhymes.

Single channelled attention*. Can shift to a different task if attention fully obtained – using child's name helps focus.*

Links to the Characteristics of Effective Learning

PLAYING AND EXPLORING

Finding out and exploring

★ showing curiosity about objects, events and people

★ using senses to explore the world around them

★ engaging in open-ended activity

★ showing particular interests

Being willing to 'have a go'

★ initiating activities

e.g. after taking part in a group activity exploring sounds outside, the child helps themselves to a beater and moves around the room listening to the different sounds objects make when tapped.

ACTIVE LEARNING

Being involved and concentrating

★ maintaining focus on their activity for a period of time

★ showing high levels of energy, fascination

★ not easily distracted

★ paying attention to details

CREATING AND THINKING CRITICALLY

Making links

★ making links and noticing patterns in their experience

e.g. the child hears the sound of a car outside, the engine stops and they hear a door slam. They move towards the door or window in anticipation of someone coming in.

22 – 36 months

Observation
What you may notice...

Does the child focus their attention when adults introduce different sounds or puppets into story or circle times?

Does the child respond visually, physically or verbally to familiar sounds in the environment? E.g. a practitioner enters the room and starts talking to others. Does the child look at, go to or say their name (or their version)?

Does the child watch with interest or actively participate in sound play, songs and rhymes?

Can the child shift their attention to a new task with support?

Assessment
What it may signify...

They can hear, and are stimulated to listen to, changes in **pitch** and **intonation**.

The child is able to hear, **mentally process** and respond to familiar sounds.

The child enjoys rhythmic and musical activities and is gaining the confidence to participate.

The child is using **single channelled attention**.

Planning
What you can do...

This links to the listening and attention section of the Communication, Language and Literacy Progress Checklist on p78.

Select and invent stories and rhymes that offer plenty of opportunities for practitioners and children to participate vocally e.g. *Old MacDonald.*

Praise and encourage responses, including naming the sound causing the response to support word acquisition e.g. 'Did you hear the gate creak open? Well done Zane!'

As well as daily opportunities for familiar songs and rhymes, make up your own based on the child's interests e.g. *How now brown cow*. (See Songs and rhymes on p138 for words and actions.)

Be aware that you may need to say the child's name or touch their shoulder or hand gently to gain their attention.

By this stage most children are able to follow simple instructions e.g. 'Turn it over and see what happens.'

22 – 36 months

Additional adult-led activities

These are additional activities or guidance to further support this stage of development.

Puppets

Puppets and props can be useful in engaging and keeping children's interest. Tell stories such as *The Three Little Pigs* with a group of four children each with a puppet. Make sure you have enough puppets or props for the children to have one each and be aware that some children will not want to engage with the puppets, they may prefer to sit on your knee and watch, or just hold a prop.

Bath time: I hear thunder

(See Songs and rhymes on p137 for words and actions.)

This song can be added to with the children as a range of sounds and voices are explored.

Home-time activities

Key communication idea

When sharing a favourite book with your child, use lots of exaggerated facial expressions, noises and sounds to bring the story to life. As the child becomes familiar with the story, encourage them to join in. Early book sharing activities are a vital part of developing early reading skills and a future interest in books.

Bath time sounds

Talk to your child about the different sounds that can be heard at bath time e.g. water running, bubble bottle being squeezed, teeth brushing, toilet flushing, hands splashing, taps dripping and shower whooshing.

Glossary of terms

Single channelled attention: can shift attention, for example from a task to an instruction then back again, as long as their full attention is gained at each stage. Touching the child gently on the arm or shoulder may help.

Pitch: how high or low a musical note or sound is.

Intonation: how the voice rises and falls when speaking.

Mentally process: to think things through.

Understanding

Early Years Outcomes

Identifies action words by pointing to the right picture, e.g. 'Who's jumping?'

Understands more complex sentences e.g. 'Put your toys away and then we'll read a book.'

Understands 'who', 'what', 'where' in simple questions (e.g. 'Who's that?' 'What's that?' 'Where is...?')

Developing understanding of simple concepts e.g. big/little.

Links to the Characteristics of Effective Learning

PLAYING AND EXPLORING

Finding out and exploring

★ showing curiosity about objects, events and people

★ using senses to explore the world around them

ACTIVE LEARNING

Being involved and concentrating

★ paying attention to details

e.g. while on a treasure hunt in the outdoor area you ask the children, 'Who can find me a shell? Where could it be?' One child replies, 'In the soil.' They run over to the raised beds and start searching for shells. They find part of an eggshell and bring it to you, looking slightly unsure. You spend time explaining that it is from a bird, praise them for finding it and go indoors to further their understanding through books or online.

CREATING AND THINKING CRITICALLY

Having their own ideas

★ Developing ideas of grouping, sequences, causes and effect

*e.g. you are **commentating** alongside a child playing in the water tray, talking about full, empty, overflowing and spilling. They repeatedly fill the cup until it overflows. On the fifth time they stop just as the cup is full and say, 'Now it's full. I don't want it to spill.'*

Observation
What you may notice...

Assessment
What it may signify...

Can the child identify a range of action words and link them to a corresponding picture?

The child understands a range of physical movements and actions, knows the vocabulary that describes these and recognises what they look like in **2D** form.

Can the child follow instructions when given in a sentence comprising of two parts?

The child understands what is being asked and chooses to follow the instructions.

Does the child respond to simple questions in a manner that makes sense?

The child can understand and respond to questions about their immediate environment or experiences. The child's **concrete thinking** skills are developing.

Can the child identify a toy when told its size, shape or colour?

The child is beginning to observe the world around them and notice similarities and differences. The child is starting to learn simple **concepts** linked to size, colour or shape.

Planning
What you can do...

This links to the understanding section of the Communication, Language and Literacy Progress Checklist on p78.

Provide different opportunities for the child to experience different ways of moving, either through active participation or watching others play a sport. Use vocabulary that clearly describes each activity e.g. 'You are running quickly! Can you stop and jump? You're jumping high!' Take pictures to share with the child afterwards and talk to them about what they have accomplished. This makes the learning real and relevant for the child and should help them to **internalise** their understanding of physical movements and how they are represented.

When asking a child to do something, first say their name clearly to gain their attention. When you are sure they are listening to you, make sure your tone of voice is cheerful as you make your request. Younger children are more likely to respond to playful instructions as they can easily feel overwhelmed when instructed to do something new.

Most three year olds can follow a two-part instruction.

Share a picture book or photographs of recent experiences with the child. Talk to them about what they can see and ask them questions, too – e.g. after a day in the park, point to the picture of the slide and ask, 'What is that?'; 'Who is on the slide?'; 'Where are the swings?' etc. Allow the child time to answer each question. Confirm with 'That's right!' when they answer correctly and guide them to the correct answer if they become muddled.

When playing with coloured blocks, ask the child to find the blue blocks or the red blocks first. Support them in identifying the colours if this is new to them. Can they find the biggest block or build the biggest tower? Playing with the child whilst modelling the language of size, shape and colour will help them to learn these new **concepts**.

22 – 36 months

Additional adult-led activities

These are additional activities or guidance to further support this stage of development.

Treasure hunt

Organise a treasure hunt outdoors and give the children simple instructions to follow at each stage. E.g. 'Walk to the apple tree and look for a red circle. What picture does it have on it? That's right, the tyres! Now skip to the tyres and look for a big teddy bear. What picture does he have?' Adding photographs of the next place in the hunt will help the children to identify the locations and will allow you to ask more questions for the children to respond to.

I'm looking for something

Play this game with two or three children. Place a selection of about five objects in front of the children, name and describe their functions if necessary, then say: 'I'm looking for something green. Can you find it, Nadim?' or 'I'm looking for something to put my drink in. Can you find it, Daisy?'.

Once they are familiar with the game, describe items, shapes, or colours and ask the children to find them in the room, and then outside. As they become more confident add more than one idea e.g. 'I'm looking for something green that I can put my drink in. Who can find it?' Praise all attempts and use any mistakes as a vehicle for explaining and developing understanding.

Home-time activities

Key communication idea

Share an activity diary for a week and fill it with photographs and short descriptions of the child trying new ways of moving or being active. If the family enjoy watching or taking part in a sport together, this can be included, too.

Cooperation

Children of this age are discovering their independence and often like to do things their own way! Making your expectations clear in a calm and consistent way will encourage cooperation. If you ask your child to put their toys away and then wash their hands before tea, turning the tidying up into a challenge or a race, you will make the experience more enjoyable for them and for you!

Glossary of terms

Concept: an idea or understanding of something.

2D form: a two-dimensional image on paper or on a screen, the dimensions representing width and height.

Concrete thinking: thinking about things as they appear on the surface.

Internalise: absorb learning at a deeper level.

Commentating: speaking out loud about what you notice the child doing whilst you play alongside them. This provides them with new vocabulary and models correct speech.

Speaking

Early Years Outcomes

*Uses **language** as a powerful means of widening contacts, sharing feelings, experiences and thoughts.*

Holds a conversation, jumping from topic to topic.

Learns new words very rapidly and is able to use them in communicating.

Uses gestures, sometimes with limited talk, e.g. reaches toward toy, saying 'I have it'.

Uses a variety of questions e.g. what, where, who.

Uses simple sentences e.g. 'Mummy gonna work'.

Beginning to use word endings e.g. going, cats.

Links to the Characteristics of Effective Learning

PLAYING AND EXPLORING

Finding out and exploring

★ showing curiosity about objects, events and people

★ showing particular interests

e.g. the child is outside playing in the willow den. A butterfly is spotted and the child points and says, 'What dat?' The practitioner says, 'It's a butterfly, isn't it pretty?' Later the practitioner reads the story of 'The Very Hungry Caterpillar' to the child. The child remembers and tries to say the word 'butterfly'.

CREATING AND THINKING CRITICALLY

Having their own ideas

★ thinking of ideas

Making links

★ making links and noticing patterns

★ testing their ideas

★ developing ideas of grouping, sequences, cause and effect

e.g. it is cold in the setting and the child asks the practitioner if they can put the 'alligator' on. The practitioner is puzzled and asks the child to show them where the 'alligator' is. The child leads them to the radiator. The practitioner smiles and says, 'Of course we can put the radiator on!'

Observation What you may notice...	Assessment What it may signify...
Is the child eager to share their news from home within the setting? Will they include less familiar adults and peers in their conversations?	The child is confident in the use of **language** to connect socially with others.
Does the child move from one area of interest to another during conversation? Can the child recall words that have recently been introduced, and use them in the right context?	The child's focus moves rapidly according to their current interests, or whatever catches their eye. They are starting to develop the emotional maturity to be able to sustain one topic of conversation. The child is developing a large **receptive vocabulary**.
Does the child point at something they would like or otherwise indicate an interest, sometimes using words or phrases they are familiar with?	The child may be unsure of the name of the object they would like or how to ask for it.
Does the child ask simple questions related to their current activity or line of thought?	The child is capable of **concrete thinking** and asks questions about the immediate physical world.
Can the child speak in simple sentences? Can they **enunciate** word endings more clearly?	The child is developing their **speech** including recognisable sounds.

Planning
What you can do...

This links to the speaking section of the Communication, Language and Literacy Progress Checklist on p78.

Allow the child the time they need to express their thoughts. Encourage other children to listen and join in.

During a conversation, notice when the child's focus moves on and gently draw them back in to the original topic. If the child prefers to follow the latest attraction, talk about this instead.

When planning new learning activities include a bank of new words that can be introduced and linked to the current interests of the children and any themes or topics that are in place.

During this stage most children begin to use appropriate intonation to ask questions.

If you notice the child gesturing or reaching for something, ask them 'Would you like the glue stick?' (for example). This will model to them both how to ask for what they want, and the new vocabulary.

Model using different questions so that children become more familiar with these e.g. 'What can we do to make the bubbles bigger?' or 'Who can help me decorate these cupcakes?'

Recast sentences so the child can hear a correctly modelled version, with additional new words to extend their vocabulary.

Additional adult-led activities

These are additional activities or guidance to further support this stage of development.

News flash!

Provide the children with a toy microphone or video camera, and support them as they ask their peers and practitioners about their favourite activity in the setting. If you have access to a method of recording this, the children will love seeing their news flash reports played back.

Parachute ping–pong

Using a large parachute or piece of fabric, encourage the children to hold on to the edges whilst you gently bounce it up and down. Have a number of soft objects ready to throw onto the fabric whilst naming them. Encourage the children to bounce the object to a named child e.g. 'Bounce the bean bag to Gabriella!'. The named child collects the object and keeps it until the end.

Home-time activities

Key communication idea

Most children at this stage of development are adding endings to their words e.g. 'dada' becomes 'dad' or 'daddy' and 'ca' becomes 'cat'. Remember that children won't pronounce all endings the same as adults and in particular 'sh', 'ch', 'th' and 'j' are difficult to **enunciate**, so 'fish' becomes 'fiss'.

What did you do?

Sing a simple song linked to what the children have done today e.g. 'What did you make in the dough today, dough today, dough today?' to which they respond 'I made worms in the dough today. All by myself!' (Works to the tune of *London Bridge*).

Glossary of terms

Enunciate: say or pronounce words.

Language: is a communication system that enables people to express themselves. Languages are based on a set of shared rules that lead to mutual understanding.

Receptive vocabulary: the bank of words a child recognises and understands.

Concrete thinking: thinking about things as they appear on the surface.

Recast: to repeat a phrase or sentence, correcting and extending it by a few words.

Speech: talking in order to express a language. Speech involves the coordination of muscles in the jaw, tongue, lips and vocal tract in order to create sounds.

Reading

Early Years Outcomes

Has some favourite stories, rhymes, songs, poems or jingles.

Repeats words or phrases from familiar stories.

Fills in the missing word or phrase in a known rhyme, story or game, e.g. 'Humpty Dumpty sat on a …'.

Links to the Characteristics of Effective Learning

PLAYING AND EXPLORING

Finding out and exploring

★ showing particular interests

Being willing to 'have a go'

★ showing a 'can do' attitude

*e.g. when sitting in a small group one of the children watches on until their favourite song begins then they join in enthusiastically with the **refrain**.*

ACTIVE LEARNING

Being involved and concentrating

★ maintaining focus on their activity for a period of time

★ Paying attention to details

Enjoying achieving what they set out to do

★ being proud of how they accomplished something – not just the end result

e.g. a practitioner is singing a nursery rhyme that they introduced earlier in the week. The child tries to join in getting some words correct, some wrong, and missing some out altogether. When the rhyme finishes, the child asks to sing it again and joins in enthusiastically without worrying about getting it right.

22 – 36 months

Observation
What you may notice...

Does the child appear interested in or excited by particular action songs or rhymes? Do they attempt to join in physically (doing some actions or moving their body) and/or verbally?

Can the child repeat some familiar words or phrases from known stories?

Can the child complete missing words at the end of familiar phrases? For example, 'Hickory, Dickory ...'

Assessment
What it may signify...

The child is developing an interest in **rhythm** and beat, and can demonstrate preferences.

The child's **memory retrieval** is developing meaning they are able to listen, remember, and repeat small amounts of information.

The child is developing their ability to **recall** words following a familiar prompt or clue.

Planning

What you can do...

This links to the reading section of the Communication, Language and Literacy Progress Checklist on p78.

Make sure to include favourite songs and rhymes with your daily **phonics**. Make up your own with the children and extended them as they grow in confidence. For example, *Copy Me* and *Animal stamp.* (See Songs and rhymes p138 and p137 for words and actions).

Provide plenty of opportunities to share familiar stories with the child. Encourage them to point out characters and events, and as they become more confident support them to repeat words or phrases. Puppets, soft toys and physical objects can be used to engage the child and allow them to experience and think about how different characters feel.

Once the child is familiar with a story or rhyme pause to let them fill in or "read" the next word or phrase. If the child is reluctant to say the word out loud encourage them to tell Teddy or a known **persona** doll. Once they have told Teddy, the toy or puppet "tells" the practitioner who repeats the word or phrase out loud, saying Teddy says 'Hickory Dickory Pig, is that right?'. Use this as an opportunity to model some possible **misconceptions**.

By now many children will seek out books containing favourite stories, songs and rhymes to "read" for themselves.

Additional adult-led activities

These are additional activities or guidance to further support this stage of development.

Group time

Any story, rhyme or circle time should be planned to meet the needs of the group. Be aware of the size of the group and that the content is stage appropriate for all. If children have specific needs or have English as an Additional Language ensure they are near you to see and hear clearly, use their name to get and keep their attention, and provide an interesting range of visual support materials for the children to engage with.

Name clap

Help the child to hear the **syllables** in a word by clapping the syllables as you say some simple words. Start with the child's name, adding significant words such as 'mummy', 'daddy', and the names of family and friends.

Whoever is wearing a ...?

Continue to develop **visual perception** skills by playing this follow my leader game. See activities, songs and rhymes section.

Home-time activities

Key communication idea

Repetition is key to developing **visual perception** and reading skills. Where possible, have additional copies of favourite books and set made up rhymes that can be taken home for parents to share.

Make your own CDs of songs and rhymes that you regularly sing so that parents can borrow them to practise alongside their children in the car or at home.

Glossary of terms

Refrain: regularly recurring phrase or verse.

Rhythm: a repeated pattern of movement or sound, or a steady beat.

Memory retrieval: the process of accessing stored memories.

Recall: remembering the detail of a previous experience without being prompted.

Phonics: a method of teaching reading and writing by linking sounds (phonemes) with letters.

Persona doll: large puppet dolls that children in the setting are encouraged to bond with as friends.

Misconception: a mistaken thought, idea or misunderstanding.

Syllable: a single unit of spoken or written word. For example, 'dog' has one syllable while 'elephant' has three.

Visual perception: interpreting and giving meaning to what is seen.

Writing

Early Years Outcomes

22-36m

Distinguishes between the different marks they make.

30-50m

Sometimes gives meaning to marks as they draw and paint.

Ascribes meanings to marks that they see in different places.

Links to the Characteristics of Effective Learning

PLAYING AND EXPLORING

Finding out and exploring

★ showing curiosity about objects, events and people

★ using senses to explore the world around them

★ engaging in open-ended activity

Being willing to 'have a go'

★ initiating activities

★ seeking challenge

★ taking a risk, engaging in new experiences, and learning by trial and error

ACTIVE LEARNING

Being involved and concentrating

★ Paying attention to details

Enjoying achieving what they set out to do

★ showing satisfaction in meeting own goals

★ being proud of how they accomplished something – not just the end result

E.g. *the child wants to make a pattern with the paint filled water bombs. They drop one and it doesn't burst. They look around and see a friend on the climbing frame. They take the water bomb and try to climb with one hand holding the water bomb. As they struggle, a practitioner comes to their aid, holding it while they climb then passing it to them once they are safely at the top. 'I'm at the top of the monster pile' says the child, grinning. Then drops the bomb and shouts 'It's a monster splat!' as the paint spreads out.*

CREATING AND THINKING CRITICALLY

Having their own ideas

★ thinking of ideas

Making links

★ making links and noticing patterns in their experience

e.g. *when sitting next to a friend who is also drawing, the child talks about the pictures as they create them, saying 'This is Leonardo the turtle, he is rescuing his friend. Look! This is the baddy.' The friend responds and starts to join in the shared story, marking the paper rapidly with a crayon and saying 'My turtle is running really fast to help you! Look!'*

22 – 36 months

Observation
What you may notice…

Does the child choose to access available materials for mark making and drawing? Can they talk about the different marks they make e.g. 'This is mummy and this is my cat.'?

Does the child add marks or simple drawings to their paintings or labels? Can they "read" it to you (telling you what it represents for them)?

Can the child recognise some familiar symbols and words in their environment? For example, their own name on labels or their local supermarket on shopping bags.

Assessment
What it may signify…

The child is beginning to understand that written marks carry meaning.

The child is developing the hand and **core strength** necessary for handwriting.

They are starting to use their writing to communicate their thoughts.

The child can make connections between some familiar words or logos and their meaning.

Planning
What you can do...

This links to the writing section of the Communication, Language and Literacy Progress Checklist on p78.

Provide a wide range of interesting opportunities for experimenting with mark making and refresh or enhance them regularly. For example, small spray bottles filled with different coloured paints can be used outside to "squirt" marks onto large sheets of paper attached to a fence or wall. In winter, these can be used to create patterns in the snow. Encourage children to "squirt" with both hands to support their **hand-eye co-ordination**, strengthen muscles and help establish hand dominance.

Set a scene or story that encourages children to communicate through pictures or marks. For example, read *Whatever Next?* by Jill Murphy. Then write a letter from Teddy asking them to come to a picnic on the moon. The children reply to the invitation by drawing things they would take to the moon.

Ensure all areas in the environment are well labelled, and that adults take the time to read and use the labels regularly. Encourage the children to create their own labels, making sure sticky notes and pre-cut cards are available and freely accessible for them to use.

During this stage the use of both hands supports the emergence of hand dominance and encourages **binocular vision***.*

Additional adult-led activities

These are additional activities or guidance to further support this stage of development.

Both hands

At this stage of development many children have yet to establish hand dominance. By giving them lots of experiences where they use both hands together their natural preferences can be encouraged. This also encourages directional awareness and **binocular vision** across the **visual midline**, which is necessary for both reading and writing. For example, use the Brain Gym® activity 'The Double Doodle' (see www.braingym.org.uk). Play ribbon dances with both hands crossing in front, above and at the sides. Hang pots and pans outside, and provide beaters for the children to "drum" using both hands.

Textured painting

Add equal quantities of flour, salt and water to thick paint and pour it into squeezy bottles. Support children to "paint" by squeezing the bottles, one in each hand onto large sheets of card. The paint mix expands as it dries, creating a bumpy pattern.

Home-time activities

Key communication idea

It is important to draw children's attention to the use of writing all around them. When out walking, on the bus or in a car point out frequently seen signs. For example, as you pass the pet shop point to the sign-age and say 'Look – it says 'Happy pets at home'. Do you think they are?'

Water painting

You will need clean household paint brushes and sponges and a bucket of water. Go outside and paint 'messages' to each other using the water. Remember to let the child give the meaning rather than focussing on any actual letters or words formed.

Sensory mark making

Pour lentils, rice or other dried pulses or grains into a baking tray and allow the children to use their fingers to 'draw' patterns or pictures. Shake the tray gently to start again.

*Activities involving selecting and picking up small items support the development of the **fine motor** skills and wrist movement necessary for writing.*

Glossary of terms

Core strength: the ability to use tummy and back muscles in a balanced way.

Hand-eye coordination: ability to use the eyes and hands together to perform an activity, for example, stringing beads, completing puzzles.

Binocular vision: vision using two eyes within the visual midfield.

Fine motor: movements that require a high degree of control and precision. These may include drawing, writing, cutting with scissors, using cutlery.

Visual midline: the imaginary line at the centre of your visual midfield.

Progress Checklist: 22 – 36 months: Communication, Language and Literacy

Name ....

Date						
Age in months						

Use different coloured pens to track assessments so that progress can be seen.
Tick 'yes' if the child consistently demonstrates this. Tick 'some difficulty' if the child can sometimes demonstrate this.
Tick 'severe difficulty' if the child rarely or never demonstrates this.

	Yes	Some difficulty	Severe difficulty
Listening and attention			
Does the child focus their attention when adults introduce different sounds or puppets into story or circle times?			
Does the child respond visually, physically or verbally to familiar sounds in the environment? For example, a practitioner enters the room and starts talking to others. Does the child look at, go to them or say their name (or their version)?			
Does the child watch with interest or actively participate in sound play songs and rhymes? Note which ones.			
Can the child shift their attention to a new task with support?			
Understanding			
Can the child identify a range of action words and link them to a corresponding picture?			
Can the child follow instructions when given in a sentence of two parts?			
Does the child respond to simple questions in a manner that makes sense?			
Can the child identify a toy when told its size, shape or colour?			
Speaking			
Is the child eager to share their news from home within the setting?			
Will the child include less familiar adults and peers in their conversations?			
Does the child flit from one area of interest to another during conversation?			
Can the child recall words that have recently been introduced and use them in the right context?			
Does the child point at something they would like or otherwise indicate an interest sometimes using words or phrases they are familiar with?			
Does the child ask simple questions related to their current activity or line of thought?			
Can the child speak in simple sentences?			
Can they **enunciate** word endings more clearly? Note which ones.			

	Yes	Some difficulty	Severe difficulty
Reading			
Does the child appear interested in or excited by particular action songs or rhymes? Note which ones.			
Do they and attempt to join in physically (doing some actions or moving their body) and/or verbally?			
Can the child repeat some familiar words or phrases from known stories? Note which ones.			
Can the child complete missing words at the end of familiar phrases? For example, 'Hickory, Dickory…'			
Writing			
Does the child choose to access available materials for mark making and drawing? Note favourite choices and ensure that these are refreshed and extended regularly to encourage further mark making and exploration.			
Can they talk about the different marks they make, e.g. 'This is mummy and this is my cat.'?			

TIME TO COMMUNICATE

Listening and attention

Early Years Outcomes

Listens to others one to one or in small groups, when conversation interests them.

Listens to stories with increasing attention and recall.

Joins in with repeated refrains, and anticipates key events and phrases in rhymes and stories.

Focusing attention – still, listen or do, but can shift own attention.

Is able to follow directions (if not intently focused on own choice of activity).

Links to the Characteristics of Effective Learning

PLAYING AND EXPLORING

Finding out and exploring

★ showing curiosity about objects, events and people

★ using senses to explore the world around them

★ showing particular interests

Playing with what they know

★ representing their experiences in play

★ taking on a role in their play

★ acting out experiences with other people

e.g. the child is playing with dinosaurs in the small world area with another child. They listen as their friend talks about flying dinosaurs, watching as they fly their pterodactyl around the volcano, making squawking sounds. They then return to play with their stegosaurus and stomp around the area saying 'dinosaur roar!'

ACTIVE LEARNING

Being involved and concentrating

★ maintaining focus on their activity for a period of time

★ showing high levels of energy, fascination

★ not easily distracted

CREATING AND THINKING CRITICALLY

Having their own ideas

★ thinking of ideas

★ finding ways to solve problems

Choosing ways to do things

★ planning, making decisions about how to approach a task, solve a problem and reach a goal

e.g. some children are singing karaoke songs inside near to the quiet area. Another child says 'Shush! I'm reading.' The children decide to take the karaoke machine outside and approach a practitioner for help.

Observation
What you may notice...

Assessment
What it may signify...

Does the child pay attention to another child or a small group of children when they are talking about something they enjoy?

The child is motivated to find out more about the topic they enjoy through listening to others discuss it.

Can the child sit and listen to a story from beginning to end?

The child's ability to concentrate is linked to their enjoyment of sharing a story.

Can the child talk about what happened in the story?

The child can **recall** and **reconstruct** the main parts of a shared story.

Does the child join in with shared stories and finish simple rhymes or repeat key phrases?

The child has **relearned** the familiar repetitive parts of the story and recognises when to join in.

Can the child continue with a chosen activity or listen to a conversation, choosing whether to join in the chatter or continue with the activity?

The child is developing their ability to concentrate and can choose when to focus on a task, and when to move on to another activity or conversation.

Can the child follow simple two or three part directions?

The child can listen to and interpret simple directions, and is able to follow them in the given sequence.

Planning
What you can do...

This links to the listening and attention section of the Communication, Language and Literacy Progress Checklist on p104.

Have an awareness of the topics that interest children in your setting, and involve the children in finding out more about them. Offering children some structured time to talk about their favourite things, e.g. through 'show and tell', can encourage other children to listen and respond. Limit the time that is spent on doing structured listening activities in line with the children's ability to concentrate.

Have regular opportunities for sharing stories and books in a small group. Provide puppets or role play costumes, and masks that link to the stories shared. This will help the children to remember the main events from the book.

Ask children questions after a story has been shared to encourage them to **retell** part of the story in their own words, or reflect on the parts that they enjoyed.

Share stories with a repetitive pattern or phrase such as *The Gingerbread Man* or *Room on a Broom.* Allow children to learn parts of the story by heart. Reading the same books regularly deepens the children's knowledge of these patterns, and enables them to feel part of the story telling process when they join in.

If you require the child's full attention, make sure you say their name before speaking to them to allow them time to shift their focus from their chosen activity on to you. Continue with your instructions or conversation once you are sure that the child is listening to you. With many children, gaining their eye contact signifies that they are listening. Some children find eye contact uncomfortable, therefore take note of other ways in which they demonstrate that they are paying attention.

Make instructions and directions fun for the child to follow, as this will help them to remember the sequence. For example, at tidy up time say, 'Quick! Let's see who can put the most blocks away and put the lid on before sitting down ready for storytime!.' The challenge and competitive element will appeal to many children, and the logical sequence will support their recall of the instructions given.

*During this phase of development many children are able to **retell** simple past events in a story or their own lives in the correct order.*

Additional adult-led activities

These are additional activities or guidance to further support this stage of development.

Chinese whispers

This traditional circle game gives young children the opportunity to listen carefully and pass a secret message on. Start with simple phrases such as 'I like dinosaurs', and enjoy sharing how phrases change as they are passed around the circle!

It's a small world

When encouraging children to familiarise themselves with story structure, use your small world area to create a miniature setting based on a current book. Involve the children in making the props, and provide laminated cut out characters so the children can **retell** the story as they play. Use junk to create a castle or tower that can be re-used for a range of traditional tales e.g. foil pie tins can be filled with grass, mud, sand, twigs, and water to recreate the setting from *We're Going on a Bear Hunt*.

Rhyme time

Sharing simple rhyming stories and favourite nursery rhymes not only develops a child's ability to memorise and **recall** information, it also develops their **aural** recognition of language patterns in preparation for early reading and letter recognition.

Home-time activities

Key communication idea

Making time to listen to your child models how listening and communicating are closely linked. If you ask them how their day has been, use open questions to encourage a full response. Many children respond with 'I played' when asked what they did at nursery or school. Try asking 'What did you learn today?' or 'Which toys did you play with?' Talk to them about your day too, so they can listen in return!

Snuggle up story time

Make time to share a favourite book snuggled up close together. Interactive stories that involve animal sounds or repetitive phrases will allow your child to join in and develop their **recall** of the story.

The power of choice

When instructing children or directing them to do something, offering them a limited choice can remove potential opportunities for refusal! Allowing children to feel in control by asking, for example 'Do you want to have a bath or a shower before bed?' gives two directions (wash, then bed) in a more appealing form!

Glossary of terms

Recall: remembering the detail of a previous experience without being prompted.

Reconstruct: to form an impression of, re-build or re-enact a past event.

Retell: to relate a story again or in a different way.

Relearn: learning again something that has already been learned, making it easier to remember in the future.

Aural: relating to the ear or hearing.

Understanding

Early Years Outcomes

Understands use of objects e.g. 'What do we use to cut things?'

Shows understanding of prepositions such as 'under', 'on top', 'behind' by carrying out an action or selecting a correct picture.

Responds to simple instructions, e.g. to fetch or put away an object.

Beginning to understand 'why' and 'how' questions.

Links to the Characteristics of Effective Learning

PLAYING AND EXPLORING

Finding out and exploring

* showing curiosity about objects, events and people

* using senses to explore the world around them

Playing with what they know

* pretending objects are things from their experience

* representing their experiences in play

* taking on a role in their play

* acting out experiences with other people

Being willing to 'have a go'

* showing a 'can do' attitude

* taking a risk, engaging in new experiences, and learning by trial and error

e.g. *Juhi is playing in the mud kitchen with some friends. She tells them they are making soup for tea and asks them to find some vegetables so she can chop them up. 'The vegetables are under the ground, you have to dig for them', she says, 'then I will wash them in this bowl and chop them up!'*

ACTIVE LEARNING

Being involved and concentrating

* maintaining focus on their activity for a period of time

* showing high levels of energy, fascination

* not easily distracted

* paying attention to details

e.g. *Zahid watches another child intently as they use the scissors to snip little pieces off a sheet of paper. He chooses some paper and scissors of his own and copies their snipping action. Zahid gets pieces of coloured paper and snips at those. He gathers his cuttings together to show his prime carer.*

CREATING AND THINKING CRITICALLY

Having their own ideas

* thinking of ideas

* finding ways to solve problems

Making links

* testing their ideas

Choosing ways to do things

* planning, making decisions about how to approach a task, solve a problem and reach a goal

e.g. *Sam has been to the fair and wants to make a model of one of the rides he saw. He looks through the different construction boxes and decides to use the cogs. Sam is putting them together in a tall, twirling tower when his friend asks him why he is making the tower spin. Sam explains it looks like one of the rides at the fair that goes high into the sky and spins people around. His friend asks him how it works and Sam shows him how to push the cogs to make it move around.*

30 – 50 months

Observation
What you may notice...

Can the child identify a range of everyday objects and their uses?

Does the child look in the correct place for a toy when given an instruction that includes **prepositions**?

Does the child understand and follow simple one or two-step instructions?

Does the child ask questions about why things happen or how things work?

Can the child answer 'how' and 'why' questions?

Assessment
What it may signify...

The child has experienced or seen the objects being used before and remembers and understands their function.

The child recognises and understands words that relate to specific places and positions.

The child has heard the full instruction and understands that it applies to them. They have the necessary skills and abilities to follow the instruction.

The child is developing their natural curiosity and wants to make sense of the world around them.

The child can talk about their understanding and recognise that 'how?' and 'why?' lead to an explanation about their thoughts or experiences.

During this phase of development many children ask more detailed questions to confirm their understanding of what they have heard.

Planning
What you can do...

This links to the understanding section of the Communication, Language and Literacy Progress Checklist on p104.

Introduce practical objects to children and take time to explore how they can be used, e.g. look at different clay tools and talk about how the serrated end is good for cutting the clay, whilst the pointed end makes good patterns. Show the children how to store practical objects and equipment so they can use them independently once they have been shown how to handle them safely.

Play movement games using **prepositions** to give children the chance to explore what the words mean in a practical and fun manner e.g. crawl *under* the blanket...now climb *on top* of the bench...squeeze *in between* the cushions...jump *over* the rope! Note any prepositions the child is unsure of and show them what these mean.

Make sure instructions are given to children when they are paying attention to what you are saying. Starting with the child's name can help to focus their attention. Give instructions in a sequence that makes sense e.g. 'Zahid, put your shoes on, then go outside to play.' This will help the child to remember what to do.

When children ask questions it is often because they want to fill a gap in their understanding, or they are trying to make sense of new information. Treat their questions with respect and try to answer them as honestly as you can, taking into consideration the child's ability to understand your response. Some questions may not have answers and that is OK – explain this to the child. Where questions can be answered by sharing an information book or looking something up on the Internet, make sure you do this with the child.

30 – 50 months

Additional adult-led activities

These are additional activities or guidance to further support this stage of development.

Crafty capers

Set up a craft activity that requires a range of tools including scissors, twisty glue sticks, hole punches, rulers, paper fasteners, sticky tape, and assorted craft paper. Allow the children to look at and use the different tools and resources, asking questions to develop their understanding of how these can be used. e.g. '*I want to stick my paper together to make a book, what can I use?*', or '*How can I make holes in my paper?*' This approach will enable the children to become the experts as they teach you how to use the available resources.

Where's bear?

To further develop children's understanding of **prepositions,** give them a small teddy bear or puppet to act out a story that you read. Include lots of **prepositions** so the children can hide the bear in lots of different places!

Bossy play!

As children play they can develop the ability to respond to more complex instructions that link with their game. In a role play rescue game the child can remember what to do to help save the goodies as it fits in with their imaginative role, e.g. 'Quick, put the hoop near the baddy then run to the tree. Pick up the truck and bring it to our den! The goodies need it!' can be followed in sequence as part of the child's natural role play. Practitioners can spot this happening, or model it when extending children's play.

Picture this!

Many young children respond well to **visual images** of the instructions they need to follow. Take pictures of the children tidying up an area or washing their hands and display these as a reminder of what they need to do.

Question time

To encourage children's questioning skills, hide a favourite toy in a bag and allow the children to ask questions about it before trying to guess what it is. You may need to encourage them to think about what it may look or feel like first, as sensory questions link to the concrete reality of the object e.g. 'Is it blue?', 'Does it feel rough?', 'Is it little?'

Home-time activities

Key communication idea

Let parents and carers know when a child has mastered the ability to use a new tool in the setting e.g. scissor control can be tricky to learn, and sharing the child's progress may lead to more practice and help at home too!

Kitchen explorers

Children are curious about how things work and why we need them. Go through the kitchen drawers together and look at some safe everyday tools (no sharp blades!) e.g. a garlic press, a hand whisk, a tin opener, a potato peeler. Let them guess what each object is used for, before showing them how they can be used, or helping them to use them e.g. letting them have a go at peeling a carrot or whisking some cream.

Practise makes perfect. Remember to provide plenty of opportunities to practise new skills and embed new learning.

Many children will be able to follow simple step by step instructions when creating something new.

Glossary of terms

Prepositions: are words that are positioned before (pre) another word or phrase and relate directly to that second word. In this context, prepositions relate to place (above, under, in, out…). They can also relate to time (now, later, before, during, since…).

Visual images: pictures or photographs.

Prime carer: the person the child spends most time with e.g. parent at home or key person in a setting.

Speaking

Early Years Outcomes

Beginning to use more complex sentences to link thoughts e.g. using and, because.

Can retell a simple past event in correct order e.g. 'went down slide', 'hurt finger'. Uses talk to connect ideas, explain what is happening and anticipate what might happen next, recall and relive past experiences.

Questions why things happen and gives explanations. Asks e.g. who, what, when, how.

Uses a range of tenses e.g. play, playing, will play, played.

Uses intonation, rhythm and phrasing to make the meaning clear to others.

Uses vocabulary focused on objects and people that are of particular importance to them.

Builds up vocabulary that reflects the breadth of their experiences.

Uses talk in pretending that objects stand for something else in play e.g. 'This box is my castle.'

Links to the characteristics of effective learning

PLAYING AND EXPLORING

Finding out and exploring

★ showing curiosity about objects, events and people

★ showing particular interests

★ engaging in open ended activity

Playing with what they know

★ pretending objects are things from their experience

★ representing their experiences in play

★ taking on a role in their play

★ acting out experience with other people

ACTIVE LEARNING

Being involved and concentrating

★ maintaining focus on their activity for a period of time

★ showing high levels of energy, fascination

★ not easily distracted

★ paying attention to details

Enjoying achieving what they set out to do

★ showing satisfaction in meeting their own goals

e.g. the children are dressed up as pirates and decide to turn the climbing frame into a pirate ship. Together they decide that they need to make a flag for the ship. They find some fabric and ask for tape to fasten this to their mast. One child uses a cardboard tube and shouts 'Danger! Sharks in the sea ahead!'

CREATING AND THINKING CRITICALLY

Having their own ideas

★ thinking of ideas

Making links

★ making links and noticing patterns in their experience

★ testing their ideas

Choosing ways to do things

★ planning, making decisions about how to approach a task, solve a problem and reach a goal

★ checking how well their activities are going

e.g. the children remain motivated by their earlier pirate play and the practitioner gives them a treasure map. The children work cooperatively to find the buried treasure. They decide they will need tools for digging, a sack to hold the treasure, and a snack for their tea. The practitioner observes as the role play develops, sometimes offering ideas or support to sustain the interest.

Observation
What you may notice…

Assessment
What it may signify…

Does the child speak about their thoughts and experiences, joining longer sentences with 'and…' or explaining their thinking with 'because…'?

The child is developing an understanding of how to use longer sentences and a wider vocabulary, which they use readily in conversation and in play.

Can the child describe a recent or past event that they have experienced? Can they talk about what happened in **chronological order**? Are they able to talk about what they would like to do next?

The child is beginning to understand simple time concepts and is able to use language to describe their memories of recent events or their wishes for the future.

Does the child show curiosity about a range of topics and ask questions to find out more? Do they answer your questions with simple explanations?

Can the child talk about their past or future experiences using the correct **tense**?

The child is starting to ask more complicated questions using 'why' and 'how' to discover more information about the world around them and to figure out how things work. They are also starting to link more of their own ideas together using 'and' or 'because' to justify and explain their thoughts. Their creative imaginations are developing.

The child is beginning to use language for a range of reasons, including telling others about what has happened. They can recognise the changes in **tense** that adults use and are becoming more confident in using these.

Does the child change their tone of voice or the pattern of their speech depending on what they are talking about? Can they make themselves understood?

The child is able to express their thoughts and needs clearly, and is attempting to vary the way their speech sounds in order to engage and involve the listener.

Is the child developing a growing vocabulary, including names of familiar objects and people or pets that are important to them? Do they remember new words that are introduced as they experience new things?

The child is being exposed to new words each day, and is growing both their expressive and **receptive vocabularies**. It is usual for a child to have a larger receptive (understood) vocabulary than their **expressive** (spoken) vocabulary.

Does the child engage in make believe play, and act as if a familiar object now represents something different?

The child is able to differentiate between pretence and reality in their **symbolic play**. Their engagement in pretend play is also developing their language skills, as words are also **symbols** for objects.

Planning
What you can do...

This links to the speaking section of the Communication, Language and Literacy Progress Checklist on p104.

Model the use of more **complex sentences** with the child so they can pick up on this and use similar sentences in their play e.g. 'Today we are going to wear our sun hats because it's hot outside.'

Show children pictures of events from the previous day and ask them to help you put them in order. Ask questions using time words (first, next, after that, yesterday...) to introduce these to the children's growing vocabulary. Alternatively, start the day by showing children pictures of possible activities and invite them to discuss what they would like to do in the morning, or in the afternoon, and what can wait until tomorrow.

When children ask you 'why?' they often don't expect a factual, adult response. Their endless questions about what they see, feel, hear and experience are invitations to discuss and explore the world around them. Show patience with their expanding imaginations and curiosity and respond by chatting about the subject they are showing an interest in. Don't feel you have to know all of the answers!

It's common for children to confuse **tenses**, e.g. saying 'I eated my lunch!' instead of 'I ate...' To support the child's growing understanding of tenses, model the correct use of the present tense by **commentating** on what you are doing e.g. 'I can see you are jumping high Mason and I am hopping on the spot. You are running fast...' Once they understand this you can model the correct use of the past tense when talking about a recent shared activity.

Sharing story books that have many different characters is a fun way to explore expressive speech. Vary your **tone** and **pitch** to create a range of voices that the child can join in with and copy.

Have regular conversations with the child, and wonder with them about why it is raining, or what they might be having for their tea. Introduce new words that are linked to topics of interest, and explore books or websites together to find out new facts that are related to the child's current fascinations.

Get involved with children's pretend play. If you join in and narrate alongside them, they will develop a greater vocabulary, and become more confident in exploring their imaginations e.g. you could say 'I can see you have the treasure now. Where are you going to bury it? Oh that's a good idea, under the tree. How will you remember where it is? You are using the bucket as a marker – that will help you to find the treasure again!'

Additional adult-led activities

These are additional activities or guidance to further support this stage of development.

The 'and...but' game

Discuss a familiar toy or pet with the child and encourage them to use longer, more **complex sentences** by adding an 'and' or a 'but' after each turn e.g. 'My cat Benny is ginger and he likes to sit in the sun. Benny is soft but his claws are sharp.' The child can start the sentence and you can extend it or vice versa. You can also create make believe monsters or heroes, too.

But why?

When the child asks a question that seems difficult to answer, e.g. 'Why is the sea blue?', turn it into a conversation about the many different colours the sea can be e.g. 'When it is rainy the sea can be grey, sometimes it looks green...'. Then, talk about the interesting creatures that live in the sea. The shared dialogue and one-to-one attention will keep the child interested, and may lead to them asking fewer 'why' questions immediately after!

Home-time activities

Key communication idea

Keep a pictorial dairy with your child to help them to understand how each day is different, and some of the activities that define each day in their experience. This can also be a good way of preparing young children for changes, e.g. if you are planning a house move or a holiday. The diary can be used to communicate what will happen and when, and will give the child time to ask questions about these plans.

Puppet routines

Acting out a normal daily routine using puppets or toys can help the child to recognise the difference between different tenses.
e.g. *'Teddy has washed his paws, he is eating his lunch now. Teddy is going to tidy away the picnic after he has eaten his lunch.'*

By 48 months most children notice when adults change the language used in a familiar story or rhyme.

Glossary of terms

Tense(s): verb tenses are used to express time (when something happened, will happen, or is happening).

Expressive vocabulary: the bank of words a child is able to use when they talk.

Receptive vocabulary: the bank of words a child recognises and understands.

Symbolic play: pretend play where objects are used to represent something else.

Symbols: something we use to stand in for something else, e.g. the picture of a dog to represent a dog or an + to represent addition.

Commentating: speaking out loud about what you notice the child doing whilst you play alongside them. This provides them with new vocabulary and models correct speech.

Complex sentences: a sentence with more than one clause joined with a connective, e.g. I wanted more cake, but there wasn't any left.

Chronological order: in time order (the order in which things actually happened).

Tone: the pitch, quality, and strength of a musical or vocal sound.

Pitch: how high or low a musical note or sound is.

Reading

30 – 50 months

Early Years Outcomes

Enjoys rhyming and rhythmic activities.

Shows awareness of **rhyme** and **alliteration**.

Recognises **rhythm** in spoken words.

Listens to and joins in with stories and poems, one-to-one and also in small groups.

Joins in with repeated **refrains** and anticipates key events and phrases in rhymes and stories.

Beginning to be aware of the way stories are structured.

Suggests how the story might end.

Listens to stories with increasing attention and recall.

Describes main story settings, events and principal characters.

Shows interest in illustrations and print in books and print in the environment.

Recognises familiar words and signs such as own name and advertising logos.

Looks at books independently.

Handles books carefully.

Knows information can be relayed in the form of print.

Holds books the correct way up and turns pages.

Knows that print carries meaning and, in English, is read from left to right and top to bottom.

Links to the characteristics of effective learning

PLAYING AND EXPLORING

Finding out and exploring

* showing curiosity about objects, events and people

* using senses to explore the world around them

Playing with what they know

* taking on a role in their play

ACTIVE LEARNING

Being involved and concentrating

* maintaining focus on their activity for a period of time

* paying attention to details

E.g. whilst outside being explorers and looking for creatures in the undergrowth, a child spots a green insect on a leaf. She calls her friend and together they look at it through a magnifying glass. They talk about what it might be and one of them says 'I'll get the bug book. Don't let it get away.' One of them captures the insect in a pooter while the other gets the book. They find a matching picture, then seek adult help to read about it.

By 4 years children will use language to re-tell favourite stories.

CREATING AND THINKING CRITICALLY

Having their own ideas

* thinking of ideas

Making links

* making predictions

Choosing ways to do things

* planning, making decisions about how to approach a task, solve a problem and reach a goal

e.g. two children are dressed up as characters from Little Red Riding Hood. One of them says 'I'm a good wolf so we can play in the house and have a cup of tea.' The other one replies 'Yes and then you won't get dead.'

Observation	Assessment
What you may notice...	**What it may signify...**

Does the child participate in rhyming games and activities?

▷ The child is beginning to enjoy playing with sounds and words.

Can the child recognise some rhyming words? Can they hear the differences between some initial sounds?

▷ The child's **phonological awareness** is developing.

Can the child recognise repeated patterns in spoken words?

▷ The child can sometimes tune into the **pulse** of the spoken word.

Can they listen and join in a shared book with their prime carer or in a small group?

▷ The child's concentration level is increasing in line with their interest in, and enjoyment of, shared stories and books.

Do they join in with repeated sentences or verses? Do they show an awareness of what may be coming next?

▷ The child is beginning to access stored memories that are linked to interesting or significant elements of what they have heard.

Does the child show some understanding that stories have a beginning, middle and end?

▷ The child is starting to recognise that stories follow a particular pattern.

Can the child offer their own ideas for story endings?

▷ The child is starting to make predictions and use their imagination to think creatively.

Is the child able to listen, focus and remember several things about the story that they enjoyed?

▷ The child is becoming more able to focus their attention and **assimilate** some of the information that they are hearing.

Can the child talk about where the story takes place, what happens and who the story is about?

▷ The child is developing their ability to **recall** relevant information.

Planning
What you can do...

This links to the reading section of the Communication, Language and Literacy Progress Checklist on p104.

Regularly share rhyming books. Play rhyming pairs games, rhyming snap or lotto – first with objects then with pictures and words together.

Play *Finish it off* first with **alliteration** then **rhyme**. See Songs and rhymes on p137 for words and actions.

Encourage participation in activities using percussion instruments, clapping, stomping, marching or body tapping to a steady beat in time to familiar nursery rhymes and songs.

Regularly repeat popular stories, songs and rhymes, giving the child opportunities to participate. Where possible, give access to recorded and written versions during free-flow. Select new stories and rhymes that include repetitive refrains.

Provide plenty of opportunities for children to talk and think about the stories they hear. **Dialogic book talk** used with skilful **open ended** or **possibility questions** can prompt the child to remember and talk about the story while also **formulating** their own ideas.

During this phase of development many children are able to remember three or four items read or seen on a list.

Play memory games that focus on either listening skills, such as sound lottos, or visual skills, such as *Kim's Game*. As the child becomes more skilful, combine the two. For example, play *Look, listen and find*. See Songs and rhymes on p138 for words and actions.

At this age children may start to tell others what has happened in a favourite book or story.

Observation
What you may notice...

Assessment
What it may signify...

Does the child point at and talk about pictures in shared books? Is the child curious about the meaning of the printed word?

The child is showing they understand that illustrations can convey meaning, and carry information.

Can the child identify their printed name from a group for self-registration? Can they identify some familiar words such as "stop", or a favourite shop or restaurant from its company logo?

The child is beginning to make a link between printed words and signs, and their meaning.

Does the child choose to look at books without prompting?

The child sees books as a source of pleasure and interest.

Does the child take care of their books at home and in the setting?

The child knows from previous experience or observation that books can be easily damaged so care must be taken when handling them.

Would the child look at a label or other printed source in the room and ask an adult what it says?

The child knows that printed letters convey meaning.

When looking at a book by themselves, does the child know which way up to hold the book, and in which direction to turn the pages?

The natural preference for looking at books in their correct orientation and direction has developed.

Does the child follow the print in books with their finger, starting at the top left, and tracing across the page and back again until they reach the bottom of the page?

The child is aware that English is read from left to right and top to bottom.

Planning
What you can do...

This links to the reading section of the Communication, Language and Literacy Progress Checklist on p104.

Expose children to a wide range of illustrated fiction and non-fiction books. Take the time to talk them through what is happening in the pictures, as well as in the text.

Go on a name hunt with a small group of children. Hide a selection of simple words that begin with the same initial letters as the children's names. Give them a copy of their name and get them to find the words that start with the same letter. Extend the activity by instructing children to hunt for their own name first.

Provide a language rich environment with a range of durable books, comics, word games, e-books, and hand-written and printed labels.

By 48 months most children understand that signs and notices convey meaning. They may attempt to read them to understand their meaning.

Model how to handle books and show children that you enjoy reading. If they see you treating books gently and with respect, it is likely they will imitate those behaviours.

Regularly introduce new books and printed resources (including electronic print) to the setting linked to current topics of interest. Take the time to read these to the children following the line of print with your finger to familiarise them with the direction.

Use **persona dolls** or puppets to act out scenarios where the child teaches the puppet how to handle and hold their favourite picture books.

Provide opportunities for the child to cross their visual mid line from left to right and top to bottom. See activities, songs and rhymes for activities where they will be required to do this e.g. *Pencil Puppets*.

Most children can follow a simple story sequence when sharing a book.

Additional adult-led activities

These are additional activities or guidance to further support this stage of development.

Communication friendly spaces

Encourage children to build their own dens and create quiet areas for chatting, reading and writing.

Instant labelling

Whenever you are sharing an object or activity that will be on display or available for children to access, hand write a label, question or instruction to place with it, e.g. after introducing some jewelled shapes in the sand you could write a label saying "How many rubies can you find?"

Marching

The ability to keep a steady beat is a strong indicator of later academic success. Participating in marching songs or rhymes, such as *The Grand Old Duke of York* or *Buckingham Palace* by A.A.Milne, will support this.

By 30 months many children enjoy looking at a range of books on their own and with friends.

Home-time activities

Key communication idea

The more a child has their attention drawn to rhythm, rhyme and the written word, the more likely they are to develop the secure **phonological awareness** that is needed for reading and writing.

Play *My Rhyme Time* – substitute the child's name, and family and friends, in well-known nursery rhymes, encourage them to join in and make up their own, e.g. 'Hey diddle diddle, Josh and his fiddle, Amy jumped over the moon, Uncle Paul laughed to see such fun and Nan ran away with the spoon'.

Supermarket sweep

Enlist the child's help finding items in the supermarket. As they bring the item to you praise them and read the label to them.

For Writing 30-50m refer to chapter 4 pages 125 - 133.

Glossary of terms

Rhyme: when the endings of two words sound the same. For example, egg and peg.

Alliteration: when words begin with the same sound. For example, the big, brown bull bellowed.

Rhythm: a repeated pattern of movement or sound, or a steady beat.

Refrain: a regularly recurring phrase or verse.

Pooter: a bottle for collecting small insects. It has a tube through which they are sucked into a bottle and another, protected by muslin or gauze, which the child sucks.

Phonological awareness: the ability to recognise and use the sound system of a spoken language. It includes intonation, rhythm and rhyme, as well as individual sounds.

Pulse: a musical beat or regular rhythm.

Assimilate: to take in and understand.

Recall: remembering the detail of a previous experience without being prompted.

Dialogic: developing a shared understanding of a book and its vocabulary through talk, and sometimes the use of objects.

Open ended / possibility questions: questions that can't be answered with one or two words. They generally require more thoughtful responses. Open ended questions usually begin with who, why, what, how or I wonder.

Formulate: to create or express an idea.

30 – 50 months

Name ....

Date						
Age in months						

Use different coloured pens to track assessments so that progress can be seen.
Tick 'yes' if the child consistently demonstrates this. Tick 'some difficulty' if the child can sometimes demonstrate this.
Tick 'severe difficulty' if the child rarely or never demonstrates this.

	Yes	Some difficulty	Severe difficulty
Listening and attention			
Does the child pay attention to another child or small group of children when they are talking about something they enjoy?			
Can the child sit and listen to a shared story from beginning to end?			
Can the child talk about what happened in the story?			
Does the child join in shared stories and finish simple rhymes or repeat key phrases?			
Can the child continue with a chosen activity or listen to a conversation, choosing whether to join in the chatter or continue with the activity?			
Can the child follow simple two or three part directions?			
Understanding			
Can the child identify a range of everyday objects and their uses?			
Does the child look in the correct place for a toy when given an instruction that includes **prepositions**?			
Does the child understand and follow simple one or two step instructions?			
Does the child ask questions about why things happen or how things work?			
Can the child answer 'how' and 'why' questions?			
Speaking			
Does the child speak about their thoughts and experiences, joining longer sentences with 'and…' or explaining their thinking with 'because…'?			
Can the child describe a recent past event that they have experienced?			
Can they talk about what happened in **chronological order**?			
Are they able to talk about what they would like to do next?			
Does the child show curiosity about a range of topics and ask questions to find out more?			
Do they answer your questions with simple explanations?			
Can the child talk about their past or future experiences using the correct **tense**?			
Does the child change their tone of voice or the pattern of their speech depending on what they are talking about? Can they make themselves understood?			

30 – 50 months

Progress Checklist

	Yes	Some difficulty	Severe difficulty
Speaking contd.			
Is the child developing a growing vocabulary, including names of familiar objects and people or pets that are important to them?			
Do they remember new words that are introduced as they experience new things?			
Does the child engage in make believe play and act as if a familiar object now represents something different?			
Reading			
Does the child participate in rhyming games and activities?			
Can the child recognise some rhyming words?			
Can they hear the differences between some initial sounds?			
Can the child recognise repeated patterns in spoken words?			
Can they listen and join in a shared book with their Key Person or in a small group?			
Do they join in repeated sentences or verses? Do they show awareness of what may be coming next?			
Does the child show some understanding that stories have a beginning, middle and end?			
Can the child offer their own ideas for story endings?			
Is the child able to listen with focus and remember several things about the story that they enjoyed?			
Can the child talk about where the story takes place, what happens and who the story is about?			
Does the child point at and talk about pictures in shared books? Is the child curious about the meaning of the printed word?			
Can the child identify their printed name from a group for self-registration?			
Can they identify some familiar words such as "stop", or a favourite shop or restaurant from its company logo?			
Does the child choose to look at books without prompting?			
Does the child take care of their books at home and in the setting?			
Would the child look at a label or other printed source in the room and ask an adult what it says?			
When looking at a book by themselves does the child know which way up to hold the book and in which direction to turn the pages?			
Does the child follow the print in books with their finger, starting at the top left and tracing across the page and back again until they reach the bottom of the page?			
Writing			
Does the child add marks or simple drawings to their paintings or labels? Can they "read" it to you (telling you what it represents for them)?			
Can the child recognise some familiar symbols and words in their environment? Note which ones.			

TIME TO COMMUNICATE

Listening and attention

Early Years Outcomes

Maintains attention, concentrates and sits quietly during appropriate activity.

***Two-channelled attention** – can listen and do for a short span of time.*

Early Learning Goal (ELG)

Children listen attentively in a range of situations. They listen to stories, accurately anticipating key events, and respond to what they hear with relevant comments, questions or actions. They give their attention to what others say and respond appropriately, while engaged in another activity.

Links to the Characteristics of Effective Learning

PLAYING AND EXPLORING

Finding out and exploring

★ showing curiosity about objects, events and people

★ using senses to explore the world around them

★ showing particular interests

Being willing to 'have a go'

★ initiating activities

e.g. *during a discussion about how to develop the outdoor play area, the child says they would like to have a den to play in. The practitioner shows the child a box full of den making resources, including a large tarpaulin sheet. The child is excited by this, and runs to their friends to encourage them to help build the den.*

ACTIVE LEARNING

Being involved and concentrating

★ maintaining focus on their activity for a period of time

★ showing high levels of energy, fascination

★ not easily distracted

★ paying attention to details

e.g. *during 'show and tell' the child shares a pasta necklace they have made. They tell the other children that it was very tricky to thread each tube on to the string, and they had to hold it carefully to stop the pasta from falling off. They demonstrate how to wear it and agree to show the other children how they made it.*

CREATING AND THINKING CRITICALLY

Having their own ideas

★ thinking of ideas

Making links

★ making links and noticing patterns in their experience

★ making predictions

e.g. *when listening to a shared story, the child asks relevant questions about the setting or characters, and links it to their own experiences e.g. when reading a book about a visit to the hospital, the child shares their experience of a younger sibling's birth.*

Observation
What you may notice...

Assessment
What it may signify...

Can the child focus on an activity that motivates and interests them for a sustained period of time without disturbing others?

The child can **self-regulate** their thoughts, and is developing the emotional skills necessary to maintain focus.

Can the child pay attention to what is said whilst being engaged in another activity?

The child is learning to alternate their attention between the activity that interests them and the person speaking to them, allowing them to focus on more than one thing at the same time.

The ELG is a description of typical attainment at the end of the EYFS. If the child consistently demonstrates elements (though not necessarily all) of the ELG in a range of situations, and with familiar and unfamiliar adults and peers, then it is likely that the child is at the expected level. Practitioners should refer to the Statutory framework for the EYFS, the Foundation Stage Profile handbook and exemplification materials (www.gov.uk or www.foundationyears.org.uk).

Meeting the ELG signifies that the practitioner judges the child's **summative** development to be at the expected level for the end of the foundation stage.

Planning
What you can do...

This links to the listening and attention section of the Communication, Language and Literacy Progress Checklist on p134.

Children's concentration levels increase when they are interested. Get to know the children's current fascinations, and include these when planning for provision areas. Learn to 'read' the children's ability to focus, and intervene with a new challenge or task when concentration wanes.

When the child is engrossed in an activity of their choosing, play alongside them and chat about a range of relevant topics. Notice if the child can chatter back without losing concentration. Add instructions that are linked to their play to further develop their **two-channelled attention**.

Children increasingly use language to share what has happened with others.

Additional adult-led activities

These are additional activities or guidance to further support this stage of development.

One at a time

Encourage the child to play with one new toy or game at a time, and be on hand to offer guidance or support if they become frustrated. Keeping background noise to a minimum can help concentration when the child is learning a new skill.

Free choice

Organising an area of the setting with resources that link to the child's current interests, and that can be accessed independently, may encourage them to concentrate for longer periods of time. Changing the available resources regularly will keep children's fascination levels high.

Time it

As children develop they begin to understand the concept of time. Knowing that they have five minutes left to complete an activity can focus their attention. Using a sand timer can help them to link the task at hand with how long they have to do it. Use the language of time to further embed this understanding.

Wake up your ears

A good way to develop listening and attention whilst keeping a child focussed on you is to use the **Brain Gym®** activity called the **Thinking Cap**, which involves gently rubbing and unfurling the ears. This is an effective way to gain the attention of a group of children without using your voice. You rub your ears as a signal for 'listening time', and the children respond by rubbing their ears and listening. (See **www.braingym.org.uk** for more information on this activity).

Home-time activities

Key communication idea

Share activities that fascinate and motivate your child, noting how long they can concentrate on these for at home e.g. if your child builds a model or bakes and decorates some buns, share these successes!

Turn off the TV!

Children's ability to concentrate can be supported by sharing books and listening to recorded stories. These activities require children to use their imagination in order to interpret what is heard, and require more interactive focus than watching television.

Glossary of terms

Two-channelled attention: the child can listen to and understand verbal direction without needing to interrupt the task and look up. This may be an indication that they are ready for class teaching.

Self-regulate: developing the ability to control a set of constructive learning behaviours.

Understanding

Early Years Outcomes

Responds to instructions involving a two-part sequence. Understands humour e.g. nonsense rhymes, jokes.

Able to follow a story without pictures or props.

Listens and responds to ideas expressed by others in conversation or discussion.

Early Learning Goal (ELG)

Children follow instructions involving several ideas or actions. They answer 'how', and 'why' questions about their experiences and in response to stories or events.

Links to the Characteristics of Effective Learning

PLAYING AND EXPLORING

Finding out and exploring

★ showing curiosity about objects, events and people

★ showing particular interests

Being willing to 'have a go'

★ showing a 'can do' attitude

e.g. *the children are shown a mystery box with an object hidden inside. They have to listen carefully to different clues and try to guess what the object could be. Listening to each other's ideas helps them to guess more accurately.*

ACTIVE LEARNING

Being involved and concentrating

★ maintaining focus on their activity for a period of time

★ showing high levels of energy, fascination

★ not easily distracted

★ paying attention to detail

e.g. *a visitor to the setting brings in toys they used to play with when they were a child. The children listen with interest to the story of the toys and how they work. The visitor passes some of the toys around so the children can look more closely. Afterwards some children ask if they can draw pictures of the toys, others are keen to play with some of the loaned games.*

CREATING AND THINKING CRITICALLY

Making links

★ making links and noticing patterns in their experience

★ making predictions

e.g. *after sharing a rhyming story, some children play a game of Snap! with pictures from the book. Alex picks up a picture of the cat and Tommy places a frog picture on top, and say 'Oh no! I needed a hat picture!'*

40 – 60+ months

Observation
What you may notice...

Assessment
What it may signify...

Can the child follow instructions that involve more than one action in sequence?

▷ The child is expanding their listening skills and is developing their vocabulary, which makes it easier for them to understand instructions. Their sense of humour grows as they spot unusual or silly plays on words.

Does the child respond by laughing at funny situations in stories, rhymes and jokes, or in real life humorous events ?

▷ The child is able to **recall** or imagine visual images that are linked to the words they are hearing.

Does the child listen attentively to oral story telling?

▷ The child is showing an understanding of social interactions.

The ELG is a description of typical attainment at the end of the EYFS. If the child consistently demonstrates elements (though not necessarily all) of the ELG in a range of situations, and with familiar and unfamiliar adults and peers, then it is likely that the child is at the expected level. Practitioners should refer to the Statutory framework for the EYFS, the Foundation Stage Profile handbook and exemplification materials (www.gov.uk or www. foundationyears.org.uk).

▷ Meeting the ELG signifies that the practitioner judges the child's **summative** development to be at the expected level for the end of the foundation stage.

Planning
What you can do...

This links to the understanding section of the Communication, Language and Literacy Progress Checklist on p134.

Playing games like 'Giant's Footsteps' can allow children the time and space to work out how to respond to instructions in a fun way. The practitioner is the caller and asks the children to line up across the room or outdoors. The practitioner gives the children different instructions to follow, gradually increasing their complexity e.g. 'Take one giant footstep. Now take three fairy steps and two bunny hops.' Add a range of different movements, and change the numbers according the children's level of understanding.

Make some time for the children to listen to story tapes or an adult telling a well-loved tale without a book or pictures. Use your voice to create excitement, suspense, and to bring different characters to life. Even a recount of a favourite activity or special day out can captivate the children as they become part of the story whilst they listen.

At news time, pair the children up and ask them to share their news with their friend. Then invite the friend to tell the rest of the group their partner's news. They can use pictures in the news book or objects to help them! This really encourages children to listen to each other and share what they find out. This activity can be tricky for adults, too!

By 5 years many children have developed a mature pronunciation of most commonly used words.

Additional adult-led activities

These are additional activities and guidance to further support this stage of development.

Funny bone!

When children start to take an interest in jokes, allow them time to share them. **Puns** and 'knock knock' jokes can be popular with young children, who like to make up their own (and they don't always have to make sense to result in giggles!). An example of a pun would be 'Why didn't the teddy bear want seconds? It was already stuffed!'

Find out more

When leading a group activity or sharing a story, the practitioner can support the children's thinking by asking **open ended questions**. These will encourage the children to listen carefully to other members of the group and will also support their growing self-esteem when their responses are listened to and valued. **Open ended questions** require children to problem solve as they search for words, and form sentences to express their thoughts. This is good for their **cognitive** development. **Closed ended questions** can be used to scaffold the children's responses, before leading to a more open style of questioning.

Home-time activities

Key communication idea

When children take books home for reading and enjoyment, talk to them about the story after you have shared it together. Draw attention to the different characters, and how the events in the story made them act or feel. Help your child to identify the parts they enjoyed and encourage them to tell the story in their own words, using the pictures as prompts until they really know the story. Children rarely tire of hearing favourite stories again and again. In fact it helps them to **internalise** the story structure and language, and helps to prepare them for reading and writing on their own.

Accentuate the positive

Children respond more readily to instructions that clearly tell them what to do, rather than what not to do. This can be tricky to get used to if your first thought is to stop the child from doing something they shouldn't be doing! For example, if your child is running down a busy path, your instinct may be to shout 'Don't run!' If instead you say, 'Lois, walk!' you are giving a direct instruction that is more easily processed by the brain. Brains won't recognise negative instruction, only the actions, so the child hearing 'Don't run' is actually processing the message 'Run'!

Not convinced? Try this. Don't think of a purple spotted banana…did you manage not to?

Glossary of terms

Peers: other children equal to the child in age and/or stage of development.

Summative: an end assessment of a child's learning or development.

Recall: remembering the detail of a previous experience without being prompted.

Internalise: absorb learning at a deeper level.

Puns: a play on words for a humorous effect, with the word used often having two meanings.

Open ended questions: questions that can't be answered with one or two words. They generally require more thoughtful responses. Open ended questions usually begin with who, why, what or how.

Cognitive: intellectual.

Closed ended questions: questions that can be answered with one or two words. They usually begin with have you, did you, when, do you, will you.

Speaking

Early Years Outcomes

Extends vocabulary, especially by grouping and naming, exploring the meaning and sounds of new words.

Uses language to imagine and recreate roles and experiences in play situations.

Links statements and sticks to a main theme or intention.

Uses talk to organise, sequence and clarify thinking, ideas, feelings and events.

Introduces a storyline or narrative into their play.

Early Learning Goal (ELG)

Children express themselves effectively, showing awareness of listeners' needs. They use past, present and future forms accurately when talking about events that have happened or are to happen in the future. They develop their own narratives and explanations by connecting ideas or events.

Links to the Characteristics of Effective Learning

PLAYING AND EXPLORING

Finding out and exploring

★ showing curiosity about objects, events and people

★ engaging in open ended activity

★ showing particular interests

Playing with what they know

★ pretending objects are things from their experience

★ representing their experiences in play

★ taking on a role in their play

★ acting out experiences with other people

ACTIVE LEARNING

Being involved and concentrating

★ maintaining focus on their activity for a period of time

★ showing high levels of energy and fascination

★ not easily distracted

★ paying attention to details

CREATING AND THINKING CRITICALLY

Having their own ideas

★ thinking of ideas

Making links

★ making links and noticing patterns in their experience

★ making predictions

Choosing ways to do things

★ planning, making decisions about how to approach a task, solve a problem and reach a goal

e.g. following a story about a rescued seal, the children decide they want to create a seal sanctuary in the classroom. The practitioner allows the children to discuss what resources they would need to care for sick animals. The children talk about the pictures they saw and discuss the pools that the seals were kept in. The next day the practitioner brings in a paddling pool and the children find additional resources (fabric, soft toys, doctor's kit, plastic fish) in the setting to complete their sanctuary. The play develops over the following week with children bringing in items from home and 'rescuing' a wider range of animals.

40 – 60+ months

Observation
What you may notice...

Assessment
What it may signify...

Does the child join in with activities linked to grouping new words by their sounds or by association with a particular topic?

The child is able to distinguish between different words by listening to the sounds they hear. They may spot a pattern of repeating sounds, such as a **rhyming string**.

Does the child join in with role-play activities, taking on different parts linked to situations both real and imagined?

The child is learning to develop **empathy** with a range of characters and how to take turns and cooperate with their **peers**. Their language is developing through talking about the different roles they play.

Can the child continue to talk about something that interests them even when others are trying to distract them?

The child is developing the ability to **self-regulate** their mental activity.

Does the child use talk to help them construct and organise their thoughts, or to help them to make sense of a new experience?

The child is beginning to use their **speech** to develop their own reasoning about the world and their social interactions.

Can the child follow a recognisable storyline when engaged in self-directed play?

The child is able to **recollect** shared experiences and stories, and **reconstruct** elements of these in their play.

The ELG is a description of typical attainment at the end of the EYFS. If the child consistently demonstrates elements (though not necessarily all) of the ELG in a range of situations, and with familiar and unfamiliar adults and peers, then it is likely that the child is at the expected level. Practitioners should refer to the Statutory framework for the EYFS, the Foundation Stage Profile handbook and exemplification materials (www.gov.uk or www.foundationyears.org.uk).

Meeting the ELG signifies that the practitioner judges the child's **summative** development to be at the expected level for the end of the foundation stage.

Planning
What you can do...

This links to the speaking section of the Communication, Language and Literacy Progress Checklist on p134.

Make available a series of pictures showing objects that rhyme and include an odd one out that doesn't match the same **rhyming string**. Make sure the children know what each picture represents. Start in a circle and ask the first child to name their picture and the others to follow. Encourage the children to listen out for the rhyming sounds. When they reach the word that doesn't rhyme they stop and swap pictures.

To encourage a wider exploration of pretend play, introduce new ideas within familiar themes e.g. if the child loves to role play being a vet, introduce some unwell magical or mythical beasts for them to cure. This will expose the child to a wider vocabulary, and can be linked into shared books and story telling.

Play games that involve remembering and extending an idea such as *My Grandpa went to market*. See Songs and rhymes on p139 for words and actions.

Select a number of objects or pictures that can be used to develop a story. You'll also need pegs and a washing line! Start the story off for the children, describing the setting or main character linked to what you peg onto the washing line first. The children then take it in turn to select another object or picture, and add to the developing tale. This can be extended by keeping the objects in a bag, each child then has a lucky dip.

Link the resources in your role play or book area to a recently shared story. Encourage the children to take on a familiar role and make time for them to share their created storylines with the group.

Children absorb new vocabulary through their role play activities.

Additional adult-led activities

These are additional activities or guidance to further support this stage of development.

Who is it?

Record children talking and expressing their opinions during free-flow activities. See if the children can work out who is speaking when they listen to the recording in a quiet area. Initially, include those who have been recorded in the group then extend by including other adults from the setting in the recording.

Audit your provision

Consider where your quieter areas are and how they are used. Encourage children to build their own dens both indoors and outside to create quieter areas for chatting, reading or writing (See *A Place to Talk* by Elizabeth Jarman, Featherstone). Also look at where children naturally gather to chat, and notice if any particular resources promote further conversation.

Home-time activities

Key communication idea

Use journey times to play simple word association games. The rules are to say the first word that comes into your mind that is linked to the word you just heard whilst not repeating any word e.g. you start and say 'cat', the child adds 'black', you say 'chalkboard' etc…

Get creative!

Make sock puppets or wooden spoon people based on characters from a favourite bedtime story. The child can use these to act out what happens – first as you read the book and later independently.

Glossary of terms

Rhyming string: a group of words that share the same sound and sometimes the same number of syllables.

Empathy: the ability to share and understand the feelings of another.

Peers: other children equal to the child in age and/or stage of development.

Self-regulate: developing the ability to control a set of constructive learning behaviours.

Speech: talking in order to express a **language**. Speech involves the coordination of muscles in the jaw, tongue, lips and vocal tract in order to create sounds.

Recollect: to call a past experience to mind.

Reconstruct: to form an impression of, re-build or re-enact a past event.

Summative: an end assessment of a child's learning or development.

Reading

Early Years Outcomes

*Continues a **rhyming string**.*

Hears and says the initial sound in words.

*Can **segment** the sounds in simple words and blend them together and knows which letters represent some of them.*

Links sounds to letters, naming and sounding the letters of the alphabet.

Begins to read words and simple sentences.

Uses vocabulary and forms of speech that are increasingly influenced by their experiences of books.

Enjoys an increasing range of books.
Knows that information can be retrieved from books and computers.

Early Learning Goal (ELG)

Children read and understand simple sentences. They use phonic knowledge to decode regular words and read them aloud accurately. They also read some common irregular words. They demonstrate understanding when talking with others about what they have read.

Links to the Characteristics of Effective Learning

PLAYING AND EXPLORING

Finding out and exploring

★ using senses to explore the world around them

★ showing particular interests

ACTIVE LEARNING

Being involved and concentrating

★ paying attention to details

Enjoying achieving what they set out to do

★ enjoying meeting challenges for their own sake rather than external rewards or praise

CREATING AND THINKING CRITICALLY

Having their own ideas

★ thinking of ideas

★ finding new ways to solve problems

Making links

★ making predictions

*E.g. two children are talking about the cakes the class made the previous week. They can't agree on the ingredients they used so one of them gets a recipe card from the book corner. They find a cake recipe and together read it, **segmenting** and **blending** together and agreeing on which ingredients they used. They talk about other things they would like to try in a cake and how it would taste. They ask a practitioner if they can try out their ideas the next time they bake.*

40 – 60+ months

Observation
What you may notice…

Can the child add words that sound the same when joining in a rhyming game e.g. frog, dog, log, cog…?

Does the child hear the first sound in a word e.g. 'c' in cat? Can they say the first sounds for words they know?

Can the child **segment** then **blend** the sounds in some simple words? Do they know which letters some sounds represent? For example; the child says 'The 'd' 'o' 'g' dog was chewing on the 'l' 'o' 'g' log. D (letter name) for dog and l (letter name) for log.'

Does the child point to print in the environment and say the letter sounds or names of familiar letters?

Can the child say the sounds in a printed word and **blend** them together to read that word? Do they attempt to read more than one word in short phrases or sentences?

Assessment
What it may signify…

The child is able to distinguish between different sounds and can add or create their own words to match the sound pattern they hear. The skills for early reading are becoming more secure.

The child is starting to hear and say sounds in the order that they occur in a word.

The child is developing their **blending** and **segmenting** skills, and knowledge of letter names.

The child's grasp of the link between the spoken sounds or names and symbolic letters is becoming more secure.

The child can distinguish between individual sounds and can **blend** them together to make words that have meaning. Their confidence in recognising simple words and sounds is growing.

Planning
What you can do...

This links to the reading section of the Communication, Language and Literacy Progress Checklist on p134.

When sharing a book with a strong repeating rhyme, pause before the next rhyming word and encourage the child to join in and say it with you. If you are sitting close to the child, point at each word as you read it so they can make the link between the printed words and the sounds they are hearing.

Make two sets of cards - one with pictures of familiar objects and the other with the corresponding initial letter sounds. Place the cards face down on the floor and take it in turns to reveal two cards at a time. Help the child to say the object name and identify the first letter sound. If the pair of cards match then keep that pair. The winner is the one with the most pairs.

Include oral **blending** and **segmenting** throughout the day. For example, when giving instructions such as 'It's time to put on your 'c' 'oa' 't' coat'. Encourage the child to listen to you **segment** a word then they **blend** it back to show that they have understood your instruction.

Sing the *Alphabet song* and point to the letters of the corresponding name. When looking at pictures or objects, model and name the correct letter sound so the child can link them both. See Songs and rhymes section on p137 for words and actions.

Play games such as *Snail Sounds* or *Robot Voice* to help children hear the individual phonemes in a word and how they come together when blended to create the whole word. See Songs and rhymes section on p139 for words and actions.

40 – 60+ months

Observation
What you may notice...

Does the child use words or phrases from familiar stories and books during everyday chatter and in their play?

Does the child choose to look at available books in the setting? Do they have favourite books or are they happy to choose a range of fiction and non-fiction?

Can the child locate information that they need from a familiar non-fiction book or computer programme?

The ELG is a description of typical attainment at the end of the EYFS. If the child consistently demonstrates elements (though not necessarily all) of the ELG in a range of situations and with familiar and unfamiliar adults and peers then it is likely that the child is at expected level. Practitioners should refer to the Statutory framework for the EYFS, the Foundation Stage Profile handbook and exemplification materials. www.gov.uk or www.foundationyears.org.uk

Assessment
What it may signify...

The child is starting to **assimilate** new vocabulary and language patterns heard through shared stories and books. They are learning to link these words and phrases with the world they experience every day.

The child is becoming more familiar with a wide range of stories and information books. They are developing preferences based on their personal likes and interests.

The child can recall where to find information of significance to them in familiar books or computer programmes. This information has been stored in their longer term memory and can be retrieved quickly.

Meeting the ELG signifies that the practitioner judges the child's **summative** development to be at the expected level for the end of the foundation stage.

Many children of this age have an expressive vocabulary of up to 5,000 words.

Planning
What you can do...

> This links to the reading section of the Communication, Language and Literacy Progress Checklist on p134.

Whenever a new book or story is introduced, provide language rich exploratory play experiences that are linked to the main theme. This allows children to develop their confidence in using new vocabulary within a context that has meaning. For example, after sharing a book about trains set up the outdoor play area to look like a station and ticket booth. Move chairs to create a long train and have hats and other props available for children to use. Leave the small world train set out with words and pictures labels for the children to use.

Ensure your book area is updated regularly with new titles and a wide range of fiction and non-fiction for children to choose from. Display books related to current themes around the setting. For example, in the small world area you may have dinosaurs to play with. Include some information books on dinosaurs nearby.

Share information books and websites or computer programmes with the children, modelling how to search for a topic of interest. If a child has a question about a current fascination, show them related books and talk to them about the pictures and text.

Additional adult-led activities

These are additional activities or guidance to further support this stage of development.

Bean bag race

Mark some small bean bags with the letters you are currently focusing on and take them outdoors. Drop the beanbags down the slide so they 'race' to the bottom, where the children can catch them and say the letter sound or name that they have.

Party on the hill

See the Songs and rhymes section on p139 for this activity which encourages the identification of initial sounds.

Home-time activities

Key communication idea

Regular exposure to letters and the corresponding sounds they make quickly builds the child's confidence in recognising these. Pointing out different letters on cereal packets, in shop names, on clothing labels and in shared story books will contribute to the child's growing phonics knowledge. Having a shared sounds book or video diary will enable the child to find objects and pictures around the home that start with a new letter sound, and record them. These can then be shared in the setting.

I spy

Play this traditional game with your child and add the middle and end sounds to give them further clues. This will encourage them to listen to each sound in a word and blend them together. For example 'I spy with my little eye something that sounds like 'c' 'a' 'r'…Use the soft sounds that blend more easily. See http://www.oxfordowl. co.uk/for-home/reading-owl/expert-help/ phonics-made-easy for ideas and support.

Glossary of terms

Rhyming string: a group of words that share the same sound and sometimes the same number of syllables.

Segment: divide a word into its individual sound parts in order to spell it e.g. 'mum' segments to 'm-u-m'.

Blend: individual sounds drawn together to pronounce a word e.g. 'f-l-a-t' blends to 'flat'

Assimilate: to take in and understand.

Recall: remembering the detail of a previous experience without being prompted.

Phoneme: a tiny unit of sound in speech.

Writing

Early Years Outcomes

Gives meaning to marks they make as they draw, write and paint.

Begins to break the flow of speech into words.

*Continues a **rhyming string**.*

Hears and says the initial sound in words.

*Can **segment** the sounds in simple words and **blend** them together.*

Links sounds to letters, naming and sounding the letters of the alphabet.

Uses some clearly identifiable letters to communicate meaning, representing some sounds correctly and in sequence.

Writes own name and other things such as labels,captions.

Attempts to write short sentences in meaningful contexts.

Early Learning Goal (ELG)

Children use their phonic knowledge to write words in ways which match their spoken sounds. They also write some irregular common words. They write simple sentences which can be read by themselves and others. Some words are spelt correctly and others are phonetically plausible.

Links to the Characteristics of Effective Learning

PLAYING AND EXPLORING

Finding out and exploring

★ engaging in open-ended activity

★ showing particular interests

Playing with what they know

★ representing their experiences in play

★ acting out experiences with other people

Being willing to 'have a go'

★ initiating activities

★ showing a 'can do' attitude

ACTIVE LEARNING

Being involved and concentrating

★ maintaining focus on their activity when challenges occur

★ showing high levels of energy, fascination

★ paying attention to details

Keeping on trying

★ persisting with activity when challenges occur

★ bouncing back after difficulties

Enjoying achieving what they set out to do

★ showing satisfaction in meeting own goals

CREATING AND THINKING CRITICALLY

Having their own ideas

★ thinking of ideas

★ finding new ways to solve problems

★ finding new ways to do things

Choosing ways to do things

★ planning, making decisions about how to approach a task, solve a problem and reach a goal

★ checking how well their activities are going

★ changing strategy as needed

★ reviewing how well the approach worked

E.g. *a group of boys were playing with some construction on the carpet, creating a seaside scene. The practitioner asked them if they would like some paper to be the sea. The boys started to draw on the long roll of paper, chatting about the sea creatures they were drawing. 'This is my shark and it is eating those fish!' 'My swordfish is swimming really fast…' The boys' ideas and dialogue evolved alongside their drawings. One of the boys accidently made a hole in the paper when scribbling to show how fast his speed boat was travelling. His friend went to get some tape to repair it and returned with the tape and a tub of junk modelling materials. 'We can use these lids to be our boats'. The boys continued to work on their developing picture throughout the day, and were proud to share their story with the class.*

40 – 60+ months

Observation — What you may notice...	Assessment — What it may signify...
Does the child choose to create pictures or make marks using available tools? Can they talk about what their marks represent for them?	The child is at the **pre-literate** stage of writing development. They may begin to include scribbles, pictures or lines that are drawn from left to right in imitation of writing they have seen modelled. The marks and pictures they make are beginning to hold meaning for the child.
Is the child beginning to separate the marks they make into word-like formations?	The child is aware of the printed word and is starting to emulate this in their mark making. Their writing is at the **emergent** stage, with groups of letters or symbols appearing with spaces in between.
Can the child add words that sound the same when joining in a rhyming game e.g. frog, dog, log, cog...?	The child is able to distinguish between different sounds, and can add or create their own words to match the sound pattern they hear. The skills for early writing are becoming more secure.
Does the child hear the first sound in a word e.g. 'c' in cat? Can they say the first sounds for words they know?	The child is starting to hear and say sounds in the order that they occur in a word.
Can the child segment then blend the sounds in some simple words?	The child is developing their **blending** and **segmenting** skills ready for early spelling.

Planning
What you can do...

This links to the writing section of the Communication, Language and Literacy Progress Checklist on p134.

Provide varied opportunities for the child to develop their **gross motor skills**, and **fine motor strength**, and coordination. For example: magic paint mats like 'Aquadraw' that change colour with a sponge and water; chunky chalk on the paving stones or playground surface; large, heavy paint brushes and water to 'paint' the outdoor equipment; finger paints and an upright canvas to trace lines, scribbles and patterns on.

Allow children to explore their emerging grasp of symbolic letters and pictures on a large scale. Do not restrict with lines or small paper! Encourage mark making and drawing in every area of the setting. Leave chalk, dry wipe markers, paint brushes and crayons near large, clean surfaces for children to practice on. Having clipboards and pencils, large sticky notes, shopping list pads, and a range of coloured paper can also attract children to experiment with early writing.

Create a rhyme time washing line in your setting and peg up a picture with the printed word as a starting point. Allow the children to sort through the washing and find other pictures with words that share the same rhyme to peg up. To develop this further, leave blank pieces of 'washing' out for children to draw their own rhyming pictures and support them in sounding out the word.

The child may be ready to match initial letters to pictures of objects that start with the same sound. This can be done as a card matching game or, to further develop fine motor control, on paper with the child linking up the correct letter to the picture. This letter recognition and matching ability also forms part of the **emergent** writing stage.

Place different words and matching pictures on the floor. Sing the *'Find a word'* song as the children walk around. When the song stops, they pick up the word or picture nearest to them and sound it out by segmenting then blending the sounds together.

Observation
What you may notice...

Assessment
What it may signify...

Observation — What you may notice...	Assessment — What it may signify...
Does the child point to print in the environment and say the letter sounds or names of familiar letters?	The child understands that writing in the form of print carries meaning. They have **assimiliated** some letter names and sounds, and can recognise these in the environment.
Can the child form some letters correctly, for example, the letters in their name? Are they beginning to write letters to form phonetically recognisable words?	The child has reached the **transitional** stage of writing development, and is starting to use the first letter sound and some end sounds to represent the whole word. Vowels are commonly missed out.
Can the child write their own name and some simple **cvc** words from memory? Do they write for a purpose?	The child is beginning to use beginning, middle and end sounds to create **cvc** words, alongside their own creative spellings. Their writing is becoming more **fluent** as they attempt phrases that hold meaning. Their writing can often be read and understood.
Does the child have a go at writing short sentences linked to an interest or for a specific purpose?	The child's concept of a word and a group of words holding meaning is developing. As their writing becomes more fluent the child begins to form sentences and experiment with punctuation.
The ELG is a description of typical attainment at the end of the EYFS. If the child consistently demonstrates elements (though not necessarily all) of the ELG in a range of situations, and with familiar and unfamiliar adults and peers, then it is likely that the child is at the expected level. Practitioners should refer to the Statutory framework for the EYFS, the Foundation Stage Profile handbook and exemplification materials (www.gov.uk or www.foundationyears.org.uk).	Meeting the ELG signifies that the practitioner judges the child's **summative** development to be at the expected level for the end of the foundation stage.

Planning
What you can do...

This links to the writing section of the Communication, Language and Literacy Progress Checklist on p134.

Label different areas of the classroom and include everyday words like clock, door, window. Point these out to the children and segment the sounds together. Encourage the children to spot the initial letter first and read from left to right. Leave blank strips of paper for children to practice their own letters on to use as labels.

Children at the **transitional** stage of early writing may enjoy copying letters and words from their environment. Providing sound mats that show familiar letters can support the child in finding the **graphemes** they need. Help the child to think about the sounds they can hear when they say the word out loud. Can they identify these on their sound mat?

Children enjoy writing for a purpose. Providing templates of postcards, shopping lists, recipe pages, toy labels or greetings cards can inspire them to have a go at writing. Be on hand to help them with trickier sounds and offer lots of praise and encouragement. Allowing the child to share their writing with others in the setting or at home adds an additional sense of audience, which they thrive on.

Encourage children to draw and talk about their ideas before having a go at writing words and sentences. Talking through their thoughts allows children time to process what they would like to commit to print. Spending time on their drawing before writing (rather than the other way around), enables children to map out their creative ideas, and can lead to more spontaneity.

Additional adult-led activities

These are additional activities or guidance to further support this stage of development.

Pre-requisite writing skills

There are a number of things to consider when assessing a child's readiness for writing, and what support they may need to develop their writing skills. They include: **core**, shoulder girdle, arm, hand and finger strength; ability to rotate wrists, forearms and cross the **mid line**; demonstrate hand dominance and **tripod grasp**; track from left to right; draw horizontal, vertical, diagonal lines and circles. Plan to provide for these areas within specific and enhanced or continuous provision. For example, to develop **core**, shoulder girdle, arm, and hand strength, encourage crawling, climbing and swinging activities. For example obstacle courses that include crawling under nets, parachutes, or through tunnels, climbing up and over ladders and frames and swinging across bars.

Boy zone*

Young boys develop differently to girls and physically they require more exposure to activities that involve their core muscles, and that enable their upper body strength to grow. Many practitioners notice that boys can be reluctant to engage in mark making, drawing, and early writing activities. Working with boys' developmental needs can change this. Offer large surfaces for drawing and mark making that enable boys to fully access their gross motor skills. Surfaces with little or no resistance are more successful in encouraging free flowing movements. Horizontal whiteboards and dry wipe pens are ideal. You could also lay large sheets of paper flat on the floor and give children chubby crayons that glide smoothly. Allow boys to lie on their tummies when mark making on large paper as this will focus the activity on their shoulder and upper arm movements.

These activities apply to girls, too!

Home-time activities

Key communication idea

There is value to be had in any marks that children make. Scribbling leads to more symbolic mark making and this paves the way for early pictures and letter formation. Provide children with a doodle or 'My Try' book for mark making activities at home. Ask parents to talk about the drawings their child has created, and add a note describing what the child has said their picture or marks represent. Dating these provides a lovely record of each child's earliest writing development.

Glossary of terms

Rhyming string: a group of words that share the same sound and sometimes the same number of syllables.

Segment: divide a word into its individual sound parts in order to spell it e.g. 'Mum' segments to 'm-u-m'.

Blend: individual sounds drawn together to pronounce a word e.g. 'f-l-a-t' blends to 'flat'.

CVC words: three letter words that contain a consonant – vowel – consonant e.g. 'Mum'.

Pre-literate (writing stage): early scribbling and drawing stage.

Emergent (writing stage): letters or letter strings with no concrete meaning.

Assimilate: to take in and understand.

Transitional (writing stage): independently invented spelling based on known letter sound relationships.

Fluent (writing stage): spelling becomes more conventional and sentences can be recognised and understood.

Grapheme: a written letter or letters that spell a sound in a word.

Gross motor skills: the use of large muscle groups such as those in the arms, legs and core, to support a range of physical activities including crawling, rolling, pulling up, sitting and walking.

Fine motor: movements that require a high degree of control and precision. These may include drawing, writing, cutting with scissors, using cutlery.

Core strength: the ability to use tummy and back muscles in a balanced way.

Mid line: refers to the imaginary line that divides the body into right and left halves.

Tripod grasp (on writing implement): three fingered; thumb, index and middle fingers.

40 – 60+ months

Name ....

Date						
Age in months						

Use different coloured pens to track assessments so that progress can be seen.
Tick 'yes' if the child consistently demonstrates this. Tick 'some difficulty' if the child can sometimes demonstrate this.
Tick 'severe difficulty' if the child rarely or never demonstrates this.

	Yes	Some difficulty	Severe difficulty
Listening and attention			
Can the child focus on an activity that motivates and interests them for some time without disturbing others?			
Can the child pay attention to what is said whilst engaged in another activity?			
Understanding			
Can the child follow instructions that involve more than one action in sequence?			
Does the child respond by laughing at funny situations in stories, rhymes and jokes or in real life humorous events ?			
Does the child listen attentively to oral story telling?			
Can the child listen to their **peers** before taking their turn and speaking?			
Speaking			
Does the child join in activities linked to grouping new words by their sounds or by association with a particular topic?			
Does the child join in with role play activities, taking on different parts linked to situations both real and imagined?			
Can the child continue to talk about something that interests them even when others are trying to distract them?			
Does the child use talk to help them construct and organise their thoughts or to help them to make sense of a new experience?			
Can the child follow a recognisable storyline when engaged in self-directed play?			

40 – 60+ months

	Yes	Some difficulty	Severe difficulty
Reading			
Can the child add words that sound the same when joining in a rhyming game e.g. frog, dog, log, cog…?			
Does the child hear the first sound in a word e.g. 'c' in cat? Can they say the first sounds for words they know? Note which ones.			
Can the child **segment** then **blend** the sounds in some simple words?			
Do they know which letters some sounds represent? Note which ones.			
Does the child point to print in the environment and say the letter sounds or names of familiar letters?			
Can the child say the sounds in a printed word and **blend** them together to read that word?			
Do they attempt to read more than one word in short phrases or sentences?			
Does the child use words or phrases from familiar stories and books during everyday chatter and in their play?			
Does the child choose to look at available books in the setting?			
Does the child have favourite books or are they happy to choose a range of fiction and non-fiction?			
Can the child locate information they need from a familiar non-fiction book or computer programme?			
Writing			
Does the child choose to create pictures or make marks using available tools?			
Can they talk about what their marks represent for them?			
Is the child beginning to separate the marks they make into word-like formations?			
Can the child add words that sound the same when joining in a rhyming game e.g. frog, dog, log, cog…?			
Does the child hear the first sound in a word e.g. 'c' in cat? Can they say the first sounds for words they know?			
Can the child **segment** then **blend** the sounds in some simple words?			
Does the child point to print in the environment and say the letter sounds or names of familiar letters?			
Can the child form some letters correctly, for example, the letters in their name?			
Are they beginning to write letters to form phonetically recognisable words?			
Can the child write their own name and some simple **cvc words** from memory?			
Do they write for a purpose?			
Does the child have a go at writing short sentences linked to an interest or for a specific purpose?			

Time to Communicate © Trudi Fitzhenry and Karen Murphy, published by Featherstone 2015

Songs and rhymes

1, 2, 3

1, 2, 3
Pat child's knee gently in time to the rhythm of the words.
Tickle your knees
Tickle child's knees.
4, 5, 6
Pat child's tummy gently in time to the rhythm of the words.
Tummy tickle mix
Tickle child's tummy.
7, 8, 9
Pat child's shoulders gently in time to the rhythm of the words.
Now you're mine
Give them a hug.

Three Blind Mice jiggle

With baby lying on their back, or sitting facing you on your lap if they are able to hold their head up, sing:
Three blind mice, three blind mice
Facing baby, hold their hands, close your eyes and gently move their hands up and down in opposition while singing.
See how they run, see how they run
Open your eyes and move baby's hands up and down as fast as baby enjoys.
They all run after the farmer's wife
Keep moving their hands.
Who cut off their tails with a carving knife
Clap baby's hands together three times.
Did ever you see such a thing in your life
Back to moving their hands.
As three blind mice
Close your eyes and move hands slowly.
Boo!
Open your eyes and smile!

Alphabet song

A b c d e f g
h I j k l m n o p
q r s t u v
w x y and z
Now you know your abc
Next time sing along with me!

Animal stamp

Start standing in a space outdoors or inside.
Fish, frog, alligator
Stamp feet to the rhythm.
Cat, dog,
Stamp feet again.
See you later
Run to a new space.

Baby Grand Old Duke of York

This version is great fun for young children, introduces a very popular rhyme with a clear steady beat.
Oh the Grand Old Duke of York, he had ten thousand men, he marched them up to the top of the hill and he marched them down again
Holding the child securely rock and jiggle them from side to side to simulate marching.
And when they were up, they were up
Lift child up as high as they are comfortable and safe.
And when they were down, they were down
Swing child down towards the ground.
And when they were only half-way up
Back to the middle, facing you.
They were neither up nor down.
Lift child up as high as they are comfortable and safe, then swing child down towards the ground.

Bath time: I hear thunder

When drying baby at bath time, wrap them in a towel and sit them on your knee (or lay them on a changing mat). Sing:
I hear thunder. I hear thunder. Hark don't you? Hark don't you?
If baby is on your lap, stamp feet up and down while holding baby safely, if baby is on a changing mat use; one hand to tap on the mat, while the other keeps baby safe.
Pitter patter raindrops. Pitter patter raindrops.
Pat baby gently with your hands.
I'm wet through, so are you.
Gently rub baby dry.

Butterfly, flutterby

Use a butterfly finger puppet or soft toy.
Butterfly, butterfly what can you see?
Fly the butterfly within the child's visual field.
Butterfly, flutterby come to me
Fly the butterfly to land on the child.

Buzzy bee

Use a bee finger puppet or soft toy.
Here comes the buzzy bee, buzz, buzz, buzz
Fly into sight from left to right.
Where is the buzzy bee, buzz buzz, buzz
Fly out of sight. Repeat from right to left.
Here comes the buzzy bee, round and round
Fly into sight in decreasing circles.
Here comes the buzzy bee, to the ground
Land on the child's lap or leg.

Copy me

1, 2, 3 can you copy me
Can you copy me and clap
1, 2, 3 can you copy me
Can you copy me and wave
Extend the activity to include a range of actions and directions. For example:
Can you copy me and clap up high,
Can you copy me and wave to the right
Remembering to mirror so that the child copies in the right direction for them.
As confidence grows, add in a child's name and let them choose the act.

Find a word

Sung to the tune of 'London Bridge':
Find a word and sound it out, sound it out, sound it out
Find a word and sound it out
Now blend the sounds together.

Finish it off

Encourage the child to finish off a sentence or list with a rhyme or alliteration.
For example:
I wish I had a frog on a…......*(child may say log)*
I wish I had a peg on a….*(child may say leg)*

In my bag I have a ball, a book, a banana and some bread.

How now, brown cow

How now brown cow, what sound do you make?
All moo.
Can you make it louder?
Encourage as much noise as possible, cover your ears then put a finger to your lips and whisper.
Can you make it quieter?
Encourage whispering mooing.
How now fat cat, what sound do you make?
All meeow.
Can you make it louder?
Can you make it quieter?

If you're happy and you know it

If you're happy and you know if find your toes
Repeat.
If you're happy and you know it and you really want to show it
If you're happy and you know it find your toes!
Repeat naming different body parts and pointing to them. Expand by changing the phrase. For example 'Stroke your hair', 'Wiggle your fingers', 'Pull a face'.

I'm coming to hug you

I'm coming to pat you, 1, 2, 3
Gently pat along the child's legs and up to their tummy.
I'm coming to pat you, look at me
Gently pat along child's arms to their tummy.
I'm coming to tickle you, 1,2,3
Tickle child's tummy at their level of enjoyment.
I'm coming to hug you, now snuggle up to me!
Open arms wide and scoop up child into a cuddle.

Kim's game

Place a selection of objects on a tray or table. Let the child look at them for about a minute. Cover the objects with a cloth and see how many objects they can remember. To extend the game repeat the process removing an object to see if the child can identify what's missing. The practitioner should name the objects to support vocabulary development.

Look, listen and find

You will need two of the same percussion instrument for each child and practitioner. The practitioner/child plays their instrument and names it (support if necessary), then puts one of the instruments in plain sight in the room while the group looks. When all children have played, named and 'hidden' one of their instruments they take it in turn to play their instrument behind their back and the rest of the group listen then go and find the same one that has been placed in the room.

My Grandpa went to market

Sit in a circle. The practitioner says:
My Grandpa went to market and bought a …
Name an object such as belt. Go round the circle with each child repeating the first phrase, any objects already purchased and adding one of their own.
My Grandpa went to market and bought a belt, and a banana.
My Grandpa went to market and bought a belt, a banana and a box.
Continue until everyone has had a go or until someone makes a mistake. If a mistake is made explain why and ask the child to start a new round with a different sound. Encourage children to look at each other as this may help them remember.

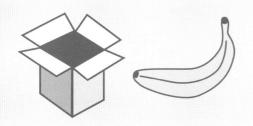

Party on the hill

There's a party on the hill, can you come?
Bring your own bread and butter and your own cream bun!
(Child's name) **will be there**
With a ribbon in their hair
What colour will it be?
The child picks a colour and the practitioner asks the children to name the sound it begins with. The child then chooses a friend to join them at the party! (Note: boys particularly like having a ribbon in their hair and giggle about this! You may need to encourage boys to choose girls and vice versa to balance the turns out).

Pat-a-cake

Pat-a-cake, pat-a-cake, baker's man
Bake me a cake as fast as you can
Prick it and pat it and mark it with a 'b'
And put it in the oven for baby and me.

Pencil puppets

Find a pencil with a character topper. Hold it at a comfortable distance from the child within their field of vision. Ask the child to follow the puppet with their eyes whilst keeping their head still. Slowly move the puppet from left to right and back again. Repeat no more than three times as this can tire the eye muscles. Repeat the same activity moving the puppet slowly up and down. Carefully observe the child's reactions and stop if they show any signs of discomfort.

Robot voice

Show the child the word along with a matching picture. Encourage them to use their 'robot voice' to say each sound and blend them together. Having separate letter cards can help, and as the child says each sound, slide them closer together to encourage faster blending until they hear the word.

Round and round the garden

Round and round the garden, like a teddy bear
Hold the child's hand and make circles on their upturned palm.
One step
Move your fingers to the crook of their arm.
Two step
Move your fingers to their armpit
Tickly under there!
Tickle their armpit.

See-saw Margery Daw

While gently rocking the child forwards and backwards sing;
See-saw Margery Daw,
.........(say child's name) **shall have a new master;**
She/he shall earn but a penny a day,
Because she/he can't work any faster.
Repeat rocking from side to side, or swinging up and down if the child enjoys the rising and falling sensation. Increase/decrease speed for interest and variety.

Shakey shakey

To the tune of Glory, Glory, Hallelujah (sitting or standing).
Shakey, shakey, shakey, shakey up and down
x3 – shake hands all around, up high on up, down lower on down;
And clap your hands together, 1, 2, 3
Clap hands on 1, 2, 3.
Roly poly, roly poly, round and round
x3 – move hands in winding motion;
And clap your hands together, 1, 2, 3
Clap hands on 1, 2, 3.
Wibble wobble, wibble wobble, side to side
x3 – wobble like a jelly swaying side to side;
And clap your hands together, 1, 2, 3!
Clap hands on 1, 2, 3.

Slowly, slowly, very slowly

Slowly, slowly, very slowly creeps the garden snail.
Slowly, slowly, very slowly up the garden rail.
Slowly creep fingers up baby's arm or leg.
Quickly, quickly, very quickly runs the little mouse.
Quickly quickly, very quickly up into his house!
Quickly run fingers around baby's tummy and up their underarm or some other ticklish spot.
For older children let them slither around the floor as a snail, then scamper round on all fours as the mouse.
Snail Sounds *– have a selection of pictures or objects for the child to see. Choose one and sound out each phoneme very, very slowly to see if the child can hear you blending the sounds together and say the word. For example, 'tttt…rrrr…eeeee' for 'tree' and 'hhh…aaaa…tttt' for 'hat'.*

Ten Galloping Horses

Ten tired donkeys plodding through the town.
Five are white and five are brown.
Bounce baby slowly on your knee.
Five ride up and five ride down.
Pull your knees up to ride high or lift baby up to bounce, then lower them again.
Ten tired donkeys plodding through the town.
Bounce baby slowly on your knee.

Repeat with:
Ten prancing ponies trotting
Bounce baby slightly faster. Then
Ten galloping horses racing
Bouncing as fast and high as baby likes and you can manage safely.

The Grand Old Duke of York

Oh the Grand Old Duke of York,
He had ten thousand men,
He marched them up to the top of the hill
And he marched them down again
And when they were up, they were up
And when they were down, they were down
And when they were only half-way up
They were neither up nor down.

Tick Tock Hickory Dickory Dock

Tick tock, tick tock.
Gently rock the child from side to side.
Hickory dickory dock, the mouse ran up the clock.
Walk two fingers up their arm getting faster as you go up.
The clock struck one,
Tap them gently on the nose.
The mouse ran down, Hickory dickory dock.
Run fingers back down the other arm.
Tick tock tick tock.
Gently rock the child from side to side.

What have I done with my shoe today?

To the tune of 'Here we go round the mulberry bush'. Identify vocabulary you wish to introduce or embed. Select relevant objects (2 of each). "Hide" one in plain sight nearby, place the other in front of the children. Sing:
What have I done with my shoe today, shoe today, shoe today?
What have I done with my shoe today?
Can Jay see?
Ask Jay to find the "hidden" shoe. Repeat until everyone has had at least one go.

What's in the box?

To the tune of 'Here we go round the mulberry bush'. You need a box containing objects relating to favourite songs and rhymes. For example, a star for 'Twinkle Twinkle', an egg for 'Humpty Dumpty'. This can be played with one child or a small group.
What have we got in the box today, box today, box today?
What have we got in the box today?
Shall we see?
What have we got in the box today, box today, box today?
What have we got in the box today?
... (insert child's name) can see.

The named child looks in the box and chooses an object. Then you sing the song together.
Repeat until all children have had a turn, or interest is waning.

Whoever is wearing a …

Follow my leader game.
The leader (a practitioner to start with) may say:
Whoever is wearing some socks today stand up.
or
Whoever is wearing red today jump around.
Encourage everyone it applies to to do the action; don't worry if some join in at the wrong times, just reinforce what you wanted the children to notice by praising a child that got it right. For example, 'Well done Alana, you are wearing socks today'!

Rhymes

The Grandfather Clock

The grandfather clock goes Tick tock, tick tock, tick tock, tick tock,
Sway baby slowly from side to side.
The kitchen clock goes Tick tock, tick tock, tick tock, tick tock,
Sway a little faster.
And Mommy's little watch goes Tick-tick-tick-tick-tick-tick –
Jiggle or tickle.
Stop!

Mix and Stir

Mix and stir and pat in the pan
Take baby's hands and make stirring motion, then pat baby's tummy.
I'm going to make a gingerbread man
Trace outline of baby's shape on head and shoulders with index fingers.
With a nose so neat
Touch baby's nose.
And a smile so sweet
Trace a smile on baby's mouth.
And gingerbread shoes on his gingerbread feet!
Pat baby's feet.

Glossary

2D form: a two dimensional image on paper or on a screen, the dimensions representing width and height.

Acoustic: the properties or qualities of a room or building that determine how sound is transmitted in it.

Alliteration: when words begin with the same sound. For example, the big, brown bull bellowed.

Assimilate: to take in and understand.

Attachments: the affectionate tie between the child and another person.

Augmentive methods of communication: alternative ways of communicating such as Makaton, British Sign language (BSL) or electronic aids.

Aural: relating to the ear or hearing.

Beat: the pulse (regularly repeating event).

Blend: individual sounds drawn together to pronounce a word e.g. 'f-l-a-t' blends to 'flat'.

Caretaker speech/parentese: a form of speech often used with babies. It can be higher in pitch than usual, has a sing-song quality and is often delivered with a smiling face, wide eyes and head movement.

Chronological order: in time order (the order in which things actually happened).

Clause: a group of words that contain a subject and a verb.

Closed ended questions: questions that can be answered with one or two words. They usually begin with have you, did you, when, do you, will you.

Cognitive: thinking and understanding.

Commentating: speaking out loud about what you notice the child doing whilst you play alongside them. This provides them with new vocabulary and models correct speech.

Complex sentences: a sentence with more than one clause joined with a connective e.g. 'I wanted more cake but there wasn't any left.'

Concentration span: the length of time a person, or group, is able to concentrate on something or remain interested.

Concept: an idea or understanding of something.

Concrete thinking: thinking about things as they appear on the surface.

Connective: words used to join clauses together to form longer sentences. Examples of connectives are: and, so, but, then…

Colour blindness: an inability to see certain colours (often red, green or blue) in the usual way.

Core strength: the ability to use tummy and back muscles in a balanced way.

CVC words: Three letter words that contain a consonant – vowel – consonant e.g. 'Mum'.

Manual dexterity: skill in using the hands.

Dialogic book talk: developing a shared understanding of a book and its vocabulary through talk and sometimes the use of objects.

Emergent (writing stage): letters or letter strings with no concrete meaning.

Empathy: the ability to share and understand the feelings of another.

Enunciate: say or pronounce words.

Explicit: clear and easily understood.

Eye pointing: using the eyes to communicate.

Fine motor: movements that require a high degree of control and precision. These may include drawing, writing, cutting with scissors, using cutlery.

Fleeting attention: being able to focus attention for short periods of time. The child is easily distracted and their attention goes to the dominant stimulus in the environment.

Fluent (writing stage): spelling becomes more conventional and sentences can be recognised and understood.

Formulate: to create or express an idea.

Functional use: using objects for the purpose they were designed for.

Gloop: cornflour and water mixed to varying consistencies.

Grapheme: a written letter or letters that spell a sound in a word.

Gross motor skills: the use of large muscle groups such as those in the arms, legs and core to support a range of physical activities including crawling, rolling, pulling up, sitting and walking.

Inflection: the rise or fall in the voice for emphasis. For example, the voice often rises towards the end of a word or sentence to indicate that it is a question.

Information carrying words: a word that carries meaning e.g. 'Where's the cat?' In this question, 'cat' is the information carrying word. A child shows their understanding of the meaning if they can identify the cat amongst other objects without being given any clues (pointing or gesturing towards the cat).

Internalise: absorb learning at a deeper level.

Intonation: how the voice rises and falls when speaking.

Joint attention: the shared focus of two individuals on an object or person.

Language: is a communication system that enables people to express themselves. Languages are based on a set of shared rules that lead to mutual understanding.

Makaton: a language programme using signs and symbols to help people to communicate. It is designed to support spoken language and the signs and symbols are used with speech, in spoken word order. www.makaton.org

Memory retrieval: the process of accessing stored memories.

Mentally process: to think things through.

Misconception: a mistaken thought, idea or misunderstanding.

Motor development: the development of muscles and the ability to move around and manipulate the environment.

Muscle resistant play: heavy work and proprioceptive play activities that provide resistance so that muscle strength is developed.

Object permanence: understanding that things continue to exist even when they cannot be seen, heard, touched, smelt or sensed.

Open ended/possibility questions: questions that can't be answered with one or two words. They generally require more thoughtful responses. Open ended questions usually begin with 'who', 'why', 'what', 'how' or 'I wonder'.

Peers: other children equal to the child in age and/or stage of development.

Peer on peer observation: practitioners observing each other, usually with a specific focus, and giving feedback to support professional development.

Persona doll: large puppet dolls that children in the setting are encouraged to bond with as friends.

Phoneme: a tiny unit of sound in speech.

Phonics: a method of teaching reading and writing by linking sounds (phonemes) with letters.

Phonological awareness: the ability to recognise and use the sound system of a spoken language. It includes intonation, rhythm and rhyme as well as individual sounds.

Pitch: how high or low a musical note or sound is.

Pooter: a bottle for collecting small insects. It has a tube through which they are sucked into a bottle and another, protected by muslin or gauze, which the child sucks.

Pre-literate (writing stage): early scribbling and drawing stage.

Prepositions: are words that are positioned before (pre) another word or phrase and relate directly to that second word. In this context prepositions relate to place (above, under, in, out…). They can also relate to time (now, later, before, during, since…).

Prime carer: the person the child spends most time with e.g. parent at home or key person in a setting.

Pulse: a musical beat or regular rhythm.

Puns: puns are a play on words for a humorous effect, with the word used often having two meanings.

Recall: remembering the detail of a previous experience without being prompted.

Recast: to repeat a phrase or sentence, correcting and extending it by a few words.

Receptive vocabulary: the bank of words a child recognises and understands.

Recollect: to call a past experience to mind.

Reconstruct: to form an impression of, re-build or re-enact a past event.

Reduplicated babbling: repeating the same syllable. For example 'baba', 'mama'.

Refrain: a regularly recurring phrase or verse.

Relearn: learning again something that has already been learned, making it easier to remember in the future.

Retell: to relate a story again or in a different way.

Repertoire: a stock of words, songs and rhymes that are regularly used.

Rhyme: when the endings of two words sound the same. For example, egg and peg.

Rhyming string: a group of words that share the same sound and sometimes the same number of syllables.

Rhythm: a repeated pattern of movement or sound, or a steady beat.

Rigid attention: the child only focuses on one object or activity. They do not usually look up when their name is called. However, they may shift their attention if they are touched gently as called.

Segment: divide a word into its individual sound parts in order to spell it e.g. 'mum' segments to 'm-u-m'.

Self-regulate: developing the ability to control a set of constructive learning behaviours.

Sibling: a brother or sister.

Single channelled attention: can shift attention, for example from a task to an instruction then back, as long as their full attention is gained at each stage. Touching the child gently on the arm or shoulder may help.

Situational understanding: when words are recognised in everyday situations e.g. 'bed' at bed time.

Sound absorption: how much sound is absorbed by materials. Soft furnishings such as drapes, rugs, and cushions absorb more sound than harder reflective surfaces such as tiled floors, tables, windows.

Speech: talking in order to express a language. Speech involves the coordination of muscles in the jaw, tongue, lips and vocal tract in order to create sounds.

Summative: an end assessment of a child's learning or development.

Syllable: a single unit of spoken or written word. For example, 'dog' has one syllable while 'elephant' has three.

Tone: the pitch, quality, and strength of a musical or vocal sound.

Transitional (writing stage): independently invented spelling based on known letter sound relationships.

Transitional object: a familiar object used to provide psychological comfort for small children.

Two-channelled attention: the child can listen to and understand verbal direction without needing to interrupt the task and look up. This may be an indication that they are ready for class teaching.

Visual discrimination: distinguishing similarities and differences between shapes and objects.

Visual field: the whole area that can be seen by the eye, including that which is seen with side (peripheral) vision.

Visual images: pictures or photographs.

Visual perception: interpreting and giving meaning to what is seen.

Vocalise/vocalisation: using the voice to produce sounds or words.

Volume: how loud or quiet a musical note or sound is.